HOW TO SPEAK
HOW TO LISTEN

Mortimer J. Adler

Author of *How to Read a Book*

A TOUCHSTONE BOOK
Published by Simon & Schuster

TOUCHSTONE
Rockefeller Center
1230 Avenue of the Americas
New York, NY 10020

First Touchstone Edition 1997

TOUCHSTONE and colophon are registered
trademarks of Simon & Schuster Inc.

Library of Congress-in-Publication Data is available.

ISBN-13: 978-0-684-84647-7

TO
Arthur A. Houghton, Jr.,
who delights in the interrupted speech
of good conversation

Contents

Contents

PART FOUR   TWO-WAY TALK

PART FIVE   EPILOGUE

APPENDICES

PART ONE

Prologue

CHAPTER **1**

The Untaught Skills

• 1 •

How do you make contact with the mind of another person? In what way should that other person respond to your effort?

Sometimes it is through cries, facial expressions, gestures, or other bodily signals, but for the most part it is by the use of language—by writing and speaking, on the one hand, and by reading and listening, on the other.

These four uses of language fall into two parallel pairs. Writing and reading go together; so, too, speaking and listening. The members of each pair are obviously complementary. Writing gets nowhere unless it is read; one might as well shout into the wind if what one says is not listened to.

Everyone recognizes that some individuals are able to write better than others; they have more skill in doing so, either through talent or through training or both. But even the most skilled writing remains ineffective when it falls into the hands of unskilled readers. We all realize that the ability to read requires training, and we acknowledge that some individuals have much more skill in reading than others.

The same would appear to be true of speaking and listening. Some individuals may have native endowments that enable them to become better speakers than others, but training is required to bring such talent to full bloom. Likewise, skill in listening is either a native gift or it must be acquired by training.

Four distinct performances are involved in the process by which one human mind reaches out to another and makes contact with it, and skill in each of these performances is required to make that process effective. How many of these skills were you taught in school? How many are your children being taught?

Your immediate response will probably be that you were taught how to read and write, and so are they. You may add at once that you do not think that the training received is up to what it should be, but at least some effort is made at the elementary levels to give instruction in reading and writing.

Instruction in writing continues beyond the elementary level; it goes on in high school and even in the early years of college. But instruction in reading seldom goes beyond the elementary level. It should, of course, because elementary skill in reading is totally inadequate for understanding the books most worth reading. That is why, forty years ago, I wrote *How to Read a Book*, in order to provide instruction in the art of reading far beyond the elementary level—instruction that is for the most part absent from our schools and colleges.

How about instruction in speaking? I doubt if anyone can recall being given such instruction in elementary school at the time that some training in writing and reading occurs. Except for special courses in what is called "public speaking," and help for those with speech defects, which may be found in some high schools and colleges, there is no instruction in speech—the general art of speech—anywhere in the course of study.

What about listening? Is anyone anywhere taught how to listen? How utterly amazing is the general assumption that the ability to listen well is a natural gift for which no training is required. How extraordinary is the fact that no effort is made anywhere in the whole educational process to help individuals learn how to listen well—at least well enough to close the circuit and make speech effective as a means of communication.

What makes these things so amazing and extraordinary is the fact that the two generally untaught skills, speaking and listening, are much more difficult to acquire and more difficult to teach than the parallel skills of writing and reading. I think I can explain why this is so, and I will do so presently.

Widespread and indignant are the complaints about the level of skill that our school and college graduates attain in writing and reading. There are few if any complaints voiced about the level of skill that they attain in speaking and listening. Yet, however low the level of writing and reading is today among those who have the advantages of twelve or more years of schooling, much lower still is the level of skill in speaking that most people possess, and lowest of all is skill in listening.

· 2 ·

In the centuries before Gutenberg and the printing press, speaking and listening played a much larger part in anyone's education than writing and reading. That had to be, because, in the absence of the printed page and with written books available only to the very few, those who had some kind of schooling—either by individual pedagogues, in the academies of the ancient world, or in the mediaeval universities—were compelled to learn by listening to what their teachers said.

In the mediaeval universities, teachers were lecturers in a different sense of the word "lecture" than the one that is now generally in use. Only the teacher had the manuscript copy of a book that contained knowledge and understanding to be imparted to his students. As the etymology of the word "lecture" indicates, lecturing consisted in reading a text aloud, accompanied by a running commentary on the text read. Whatever the students learned, they learned by listening, and the better they were able to listen, the more they were able to learn.

In the great mediaeval universities of Oxford and Cambridge, Paris, Padua, and Cologne, basic schooling involved training in the arts or skills that were first called "liberal arts" by the ancients. These arts included the various skills in dealing with language, on the one hand, and in dealing with operations and symbolism of mathematics, on the other hand.

Plato and Aristotle thought, and the mediaeval universities followed them in thinking, that the arts of grammar, rhetoric, and logic were the skills that had to be acquired for learning how to use language effectively in writing and reading, in speaking and listening. The arts that had to be acquired for learning how to measure, calculate, and estimate went by the names of arithmetic, geometry, music, and astronomy.

These were the seven liberal arts in which mediaeval

students were supposed to acquire proficiency in order to become certified as bachelors of art. The word "bachelor" did not mean that they were unwed males, not yet initiated into the mysteries of marriage. On the contrary, it meant that they were sufficiently initiated into the world of learning to go on studying in the higher levels of the university, in the faculties of law, medicine, or theology.

The B.A. degree was a certificate of initiation, a passport into the world of higher learning. It did not signify that those thus certified were learned, but only that they had become competent as learners by virtue of having acquired the skills of learning—skills in the use of language and in the use of other symbols.

Most people today who use the phrase "liberal arts" or refer to liberal education do not have the faintest notion of what the liberal arts once were or the role they played in ancient and mediaeval education at the level that we would today call basic schooling.

One reason for this is that, in the course of modern times, the liberal arts have all but disappeared from the course of study.

Anyone who looks up the curriculum of the educational institutions in this country in the eighteenth century will find that it included instruction in grammar, rhetoric, and logic, still conceived as arts or skills in the use of language—skills in writing and speaking and also reading, if not in listening.

By the end of the nineteenth century, grammar still remained, but rhetoric and logic were no longer part of basic schooling, and in our own century, instruction in grammar has dwindled away, though vestiges of it may still remain here and there.

The liberal arts as recognized elements in basic school-

ing have been replaced by instruction in English. It is the
so-called English teacher who gives elementary instruction
in reading and elementary and more advanced instruction
in composition. Unfortunately, the latter usually lays much
more stress on what is called "creative writing" than it does
on writing that tries to convey thought—ideas, knowledge, or understanding. Some students receive instruction
in public speaking, but this falls far short of training in all
the skills required for effective speech. None, as I have
said before, receives any instruction in listening.

· 3 ·

Those who complain about the low level of skill in writing and reading that is now attained by most graduates of
our schools and colleges make the mistake of assuming that
if these deficiencies were remedied, all would be well. They
assume that, if a person has learned to write well and read
well, he* will of course know how to speak well and listen
well. That is simply not the case.

The reason why is that speaking and listening differ in
remarkable ways from writing and reading. Their difference makes it much more difficult to acquire the requisite
skills. Let me explain.

On the surface, it would appear that speaking and listening perfectly parallel writing and reading. Both pairs
involve uses of language whereby one mind reaches out to
another and that other responds. If one can do this well

---

*The reader should be advised that when I use the word "man" or the mas-
culine pronouns "he" or "him," I am referring to all human beings, both male
and female, not just males. I do not always use "he" and "him" instead of "he
and she" or "him and her," my choice of which to use in a given sentence being
determined solely by stylistic considerations.

by means of the written word, why should there be any more difficulty in doing it well by means of the spoken word? If one can respond well to the written word, why cannot one respond as well to the spoken word?

The fluidity and fluency of oral discourse is the reason why that is not so. One is always able to go back over what one has read, read it again, and make a better job of it. One can improve one's reading endlessly, by reading something over and over again. I have done this in my own reading of the great books.

In writing, one is always able to revise and improve what one has written. No writer need pass on a piece of writing to someone else until he or she is satisfied that it is written as well as possible. That, too, has been part of my own experience in writing books or anything else.

In the case of both reading and writing, the essential element in the requisite skill consists in knowing how to improve one's reading or writing. That essential element plays no part in the skill to be attained in speaking and listening, because speaking and listening are transient and fleeting like performing arts, as writing and reading are not. The latter are more like painting and sculpture, the products of which have permanence.

Consider such performing arts as acting, ballet dancing, playing a musical instrument, or conducting an orchestra. In all of these, a given performance, once it is given, cannot be improved. The artist may be able to improve *on* it in a later performance, but during the time he or she is on stage, that one performance should be as good as it can be made. When the curtain goes down it is finished—unamendable.

The situation is exactly the same in speaking and listening. One cannot go back over what one is saying orally and improve it, as one can go back over what one has written and improve it. Unlike writing, ongoing speech is generally unamendable. Any effort to take back what one has said while one is speaking often turns out to be more confusing than letting the deficiencies stand.

A prepared speech is, of course, amendable before being delivered, as a piece of writing is. An impromptu or improvised speech is not.

One may be able to do a better job of speaking at some later time, but on a particular occasion, whatever excellence one is able to achieve must be achieved right then and there. Similarly, there is no way of improving one's listening on a given occasion. It has to be as good as it can be right then and there.

A writer can at least hope that readers will take as much time as may be necessary to understand the written message, but the speaker cannot cherish any such hope. He or she must contrive what is to be said in such a way that it is as understandable as possible the first time around. The time span of speaking and listening coincide. Both begin and end together. Not so the time spans of writing and reading.

· 4 ·

All of these differences between reading and writing, on the one hand, and listening and speaking, on the other, may be the reason why I did not immediately follow up *How to Read a Book* with a companion volume on how to listen. I have put off that much harder task for more than forty years, but I think I should do so no longer, because I have become so aware of the almost universal defects in listening that are manifested on all sides.

It is possible to set forth the rules and directions for reading well without including rules and directions for writing well. That is what I did in *How to Read a Book*, and it was justified by the fact that I was then mainly concerned with reading the very best books, which are, of course, all well written.

When we turn from written to oral discourse, we are confronted with a different state of affairs. One can deal with writing and reading separately; in fact, that is the way they are dealt with in our schools. That is not possible in the case of speaking and listening, if for no other reason than the fact that the most important kind of speaking and listening occurs in talk or conversation, which is a two-way affair that involves us as both speakers and listeners.

It is possible to deal with uninterrupted speech by itself. Skill in that performance can be acquired without skill in listening. So, too, is it possible to deal with silent listening by itself. Skill in that performance can be acquired without skill in speaking. But it is impossible to acquire skill in conversation—in talk or discussion—without learning how to speak and how to listen well.

CHAPTER II

The Solitary and the Social

· I ·

Our dealing with the minds of others can be either solitary or social. Our use of free time for the pursuits of leisure can be similarly divided. We engage in them either entirely alone or in the company of others and with their cooperation.

It would appear that the use of one's mind to deal with the minds of others would always turn out to be social rather than solitary. Solitary uses of the mind would appear to be confined to those uses that do not involve another mind, as when we study the phenomena of nature, examine the institutions of the society in which we live, or explore the past and speculate about the future.

But, of course, reading and writing can be done in a solitary fashion, and they usually are—in the solitude of one's study, at one's desk, or in one's armchair. The fact that in writing we are addressing ourselves to the minds of others does not make the writing itself a social affair. The same is true of reading. Getting at the mind of the writer through the words he or she has put on paper does not make reading a social event.

In contrast to writing and reading, which are usually solitary undertakings, speaking and listening are always social and cannot be otherwise. They always involve human confrontations. They usually involve the physical presence of other persons, the speaker speaking to listeners who are present while he or she speaks, the listener listening to a speaker who is right there. This is one of the things that makes speaking and listening more complex than writing and reading—and more difficult to control for the sake of rendering them more effective.

While they are always social, the social aspect of speaking and listening may be aborted or consummated. It is aborted when the confrontation of speaker and listener involves the suppression of one or the other. When that happens you have uninterrupted speech and silent listening. It's something like a one-way street, with all the traffic going in one direction.

You have the same result when someone addresses a public audience, when someone reports to a board of directors or to a committee, when teachers give lectures to students, when candidates for public office make formal speeches to the electorate, and when someone holds forth at a dinner party, monopolizing everyone's attention for a time. These are all varieties of the one-way street.

That public addresses, lectures, and political speeches can now be made uninterruptedly to a silently listening audience widely dispersed by means of television changes the picture in only one way. When the silent listeners of uninterrupted speech are physically present in the same place as the speaker, there is always the possibility that the one-way street can be opened up for traffic in both directions—the silent listener asking the speaker questions or commenting on what has been said to elicit some response. That cannot happen when the silent listeners are sitting in front of the television screen.

The social aspect of speaking and listening is consummated rather than aborted when uninterrupted speech and silent listening are replaced by talk, discussion, or conversation. All three of the words I have just used—"talk," "discussion," and "conversation"—have enough common meaning to be almost interchangeable. What is common to all three is the two-way traffic in which individuals are both speakers and listeners, alternating from one role to the other.

· 2 ·

When I first thought of writing this book, I was going to entitle it *How to Talk and How to Listen*. I soon realized that while talking always involves speaking, the reverse was not the case. We speak *to* others, but when our speaking involves us also in listening to what they have to say, we are engaged in talking *with* them. We say "Let's talk together," never "Let's speak together."

The word "talk" is sometimes misused as a synonym for "speech," as when someone says "I was asked to give a talk" instead of saying "I was asked to give a speech." Strictly speaking, you cannot give a talk. You can have one, but only if someone else talks with you. You can give a speech even if the audience that is physically present only appears to be listening to you.

The word "discussion" escapes such misuses. We always use it to refer to the two-way traffic of alternating interchanges between speakers and listeners.

The one difference between the meaning of the word "discussion" and the meaning of "conversation" lies in the notion that a discussion is a conversation carried on with a definite and even stated purpose and that it is guided or controlled in some way to achieve the goal that has been set. While all discussions are conversations, not all conversations are discussions, for they are often carried on with no particular objective and with little or no direction or control.

"Conversation" is the word I shall use most frequently because it has the widest application, covering highly purposeful and controlled discussions at one end of the spectrum (including even formal debates or disputations) and the idlest of talk at the other end (such as cocktail chatter or what we sometimes call small talk).

"Communication" is the jargon word of the social scientists and of electronics specialists who have developed elaborate "communication theories." Fortunately, there is no "conversation theory," and that is why I much prefer "conversation" to "communication."

There is communication among brute animals in a wide variety of ways, but no conversation. There is even a sense in which any physical thing that sends a signal to another physical thing that receives it and responds to it in some way can be said to be in communication. But the sending and receiving of signals is not conversation, talk, or discussion. Brutes do not talk with one another; they do not carry on discussions.

The one aspect of communication that I wish to preserve in my consideration of conversation is the notion of community that it involves. Without communication, there can be no community. Human beings cannot form a community or share in a common life without communicating with one another.

That is why conversation, discussion, or talk is the most

important form of speaking and listening. If the social aspect of speaking and listening were always aborted, as is the case in uninterrupted speech and silent listening, there would be little or no community among speakers and listeners. A lively and flourishing community of human beings requires that the social aspect of their speaking and listening be consummated rather than aborted.

In several respects, written discourse parallels the two-way traffic of conversation: in sustained correspondence between persons who write letters to one another that genuinely respond to what the other person has written; and in polemical interchanges, as when an author challenges an adverse review of his book and elicits a rejoinder from the critic.

· 3 ·

The three main parts of this book accord with the threefold way in which I have divided up speaking and listening. Part Two will deal with uninterrupted speech; Part Three with silent listening; and Part Four with conversation. Of these three, the third is both the most important and the most difficult for human beings to do well.

Conversation may be playful as well as purposeful, and it may turn from being one to being the other. When playful it may be relatively mindless, as it usually is in idle chitchat. Even when playful, it may be mindful of ideas and rich with insights.

Sometimes conversation is relatively uncontrolled, as at dinner parties or in drawing rooms, and sometimes it is highly controlled, as in business negotiations, business meetings, conferences of all sorts, political debate, academic disputations, church synods, councils, or other ecclesiastical conclaves, and in the kind of teaching, so rare today, that consists in carrying on discussion.

· 4 ·

I said at the beginning of this chapter that the use of our free time for the pursuits of leisure can be divided into the solitary and the social. Cooking, carpentry, gardening, when done for pleasure (the satisfaction of work well done), not for profit, are examples of solitary leisure pursuits. So, too, are writing and reading, looking at pictures, listening to music, travelling and observing, and above all, thinking.

The leisure pursuits that are preeminently social include all acts of friendship and, above all, conversation in its many forms. In my judgment, engaging in good conversation—talk that is both enjoyable and rewarding—is one of the very best uses that human beings can make of their free time. It brings to fruition much that has been gained through other leisure pursuits. It is their true fulfillment.

That is why it is so important for human beings to enrich their lives by having both the skill that is required for engaging in good conversation and also the will and motivation that impels them to devote much of their free time to it, replacing many of the things that they now resort to in order to fill empty time.

PART TWO
Uninterrupted Speech

CHAPTER **III**

"That's Just Rhetoric!"

· I ·

Shortly after the explosion of the first atomic bombs, President Hutchins of the University of Chicago instituted a Committee to Frame a World Constitution. Among the eminent persons who composed the group were two men of quite opposite temperaments—one, the Professor of Italian Literature at the University, himself a poet of renown, Guiseppe Antonio Borgese; the other, James Landis, the staid, prosaic, matter of fact Dean of the Harvard Law School.

On one occasion at which I was present, Professor Borgese addressed his colleagues on a subject dear to his heart. As he warmed to his subject, his voice rose, his eyes flashed, and his language became more and more forceful, reaching a crescendo of poetry and passion that left all of us spellbound—all except one. In the moment of silence that ensued, Dean Landis fixed Borgese with a cold stare and said in a low voice, "That's just rhetoric!" Borgese, equally cold but with anger, and pointing a finger at Landis that might have been a pistol, replied: "When you say that again, smile!"

21]

What did Dean Landis mean by his remark? What could he have meant?

Certainly not that Borgese's speech was ungrammatical and illogical, leaving it no qualities of utterance at all except those which were rhetorical. Though English was not his native tongue, Professor Borgese was a master of the language. From having engaged in many arguments with him, I can vouch for his analytical prowess and the cogency of his reasoning. He had a flair for embellishing his remarks with imagery, with metaphors, with well-timed pauses and staccato outbursts that riveted attention on what he was saying and drove home the points he was trying to make.

Therein lay the rhetorical power of his address, a power that the equally well-phrased and well-reasoned remarks of the reserved Anglo-Saxon Dean of the Harvard Law School almost always lacked. Why did the Dean object to this quality in his Italian colleague's utterance? What was wrong with it? He may have restrained himself from resorting to the devices so skillfully employed by Professor Borgese, but their temperamental difference in style did not justify his dismissing the speech of Borgese as "just rhetoric."

To put the best face on the criticism that Dean Landis levelled at Professor Borgese, we must interpret it as meaning not that the latter's oration was *just* rhetoric, but rather that it was *more* rhetorical than the occasion required.

Borgese was not on a platform addressing a large audience of strangers, whom he was trying to persuade. He was sitting around a table with colleagues who were engaged with him in an undertaking the underlying presuppositions of which they all shared. The issue under consideration called for the examination of a wide assortment of facts and the weighing of many reasons pro and con.

That, in the view of Dean Landis, could only be done well by sticking, closely and coolly, to the pertinent matters, eschewing all irrelevant digressions that added more heat than light to the discussion. Hence his curt rebuff to Borgese that, in effect, said: "Cut the unnecessary rhetoric out!"

Unnecessary because it was too much for this particular occasion? Or unnecessary because it is never needed at all? It can hardly be the latter. To think so amounts to thinking that speaking grammatically and logically always suffices for the purpose at hand. That it almost never does. One might just as well say that speaking to others never requires any consideration of how to get them to listen to what you have to say or how to make what you have to say affect their minds and hearts in ways that you wish to achieve.

Grammar, logic, and rhetoric are the three arts concerned with excellence in the use of language for the expression of thought and feeling. The first two of them may suffice for putting one's thoughts and feelings down on paper as a private memorandum to file away for future reference. We do not need the skills of rhetoric in talking to ourselves or in making a written record for our own use. We seldom if ever have to persuade ourselves that our thinking should be harkened to and adopted or that our sentiments are well-grounded and should be shared. But if we ever stand in need of persuading ourselves that we are on the right track, then just being grammatical and logical in our soliloquizing or note-making will not be enough. We must do something more to win our own commitment to the conclusion reached or the sentiment proposed. As we sometimes say, we have to "talk ourselves into it." That is where rhetoric comes in.

Rare as the need for rhetoric may be when we are speaking only to ourselves, we are unlikely to be able to do without it when we are speaking to others. The reason is clear. We almost always have to try to persuade them not only to listen to what we have to say, but also to agree with us and to think or act accordingly.

· 2 ·

The ancient and honorable art of rhetoric is the art of persuasion. Along with grammar and logic, it has held an important place in education for almost twenty-five centuries. That place was much more important in Greek and Roman antiquity, when an educated person was expected to be something of an orator, and also in the seventeenth and eighteenth centuries, when emphasis was laid not just on substance but on style in speech and writing.

These arts have all but vanished in the basic schooling of the young today. Of the three, rhetoric is the one most strikingly absent from the first twelve years of education. A few of those going on to college may take courses in public speaking, but most have not been trained in the skills of persuasion.

Throughout its long history, the teaching of rhetoric has been concerned mainly, if not exclusively, with oratory and with style. Style in the use of language, style that makes the communication of substance either more elegant or more effective, is a quality common to both the written and the spoken word. Whether or not elegance is always desirable, it may not always render the communication more effective as an effort at persuasion.

Since our interest in rhetoric is concerned with effective persuasion in speaking to others, we cannot help being struck by the fact that, in its long history, rhetoric has been so closely, if not exclusively, associated with oratory. Many books on the subject—for example, a famous one by Quintilian, a Roman master of the art—use the word "oratory" in their titles rather than the word "rhetoric." In antiquity and early modern times, the descriptive epithet "orator" was interchangeable with "rhetorician."

What's wrong with this? Simply that oratory consists of attempts to persuade others to act in one way or another. The rhetorical skill of the orator is aimed solely at a practical result, either a course of action to be adopted, a value judgment to be made, or an attitude to be taken toward another person or group of persons.

A practical result, however, is not the sole use of rhetoric, not even its most frequent or most important application. We are as frequently concerned with moving the mind of someone else to think as we do. That is often as important to us as moving someone else to act or feel as we wish them to. Our rhetorical aim then is purely intellectual, one might almost say theoretical, rather than practical. When we try to exert our rhetorical skill for this purpose, we are persuaders of a different kind than when we engage in oratory for a practical purpose.

The trouble with "oratory" as the name for the practical use of rhetoric in speaking to others is that it smacks too much of the political platform, the court room, or the legislative assembly. Politics is not the only arena in which human beings need rhetorical skill. They need it in business. They need it in any enterprise in which they are engaged *with* others or *against* others in attempting to achieve some practical result.

In all these areas, as well as in politics, we may find ourselves trying to sell something to someone else. Practical persuasion in all its myriad forms is salesmanship. I am, therefore, going to adopt the lowly phrase "sales talk" as the name for the kind of speaking to others that involves persuasion with an eye on some practical result to be achieved.

What name, then, shall we adopt for the other kind of speaking to others, the kind that involves persuasion with an eye on some purely intellectual or theoretical result? Teaching? Instruction? Yes, though it should be remembered that instruction takes many forms. Sometimes the teacher is not simply a speaker addressing an audience that consists of silent listeners. When teachers perform that way, they teach by telling rather than by asking. Teaching by telling is lecturing, and good lecturers are just as much concerned with persuading listeners as good salespeople are.

Though persuasion is involved in both instruction and selling, the one for a purely theoretical or intellectual result, the other for a practical result, I think it most convenient to adopt the following terminology. I will refer to all attempts to achieve a practical result as "persuasive speech," and all attempts to achieve a change of mind (without any regard to action) as "instructive speech." What I have called the "sales talk" is persuasive speech. The lecture is instructive speech.

I shall discuss these two main types of uninterrupted speech before I consider special variants of each of them: in the next chapter, the sales talk; and in the one following, the lecture.

· 3 ·

Such terms as "sales talk," "persuasion," and even "rhetoric" carry invidious connotations for those who think that to engage in selling, in persuasion, or in the use of rhetorical devices is to indulge in sophistry.

Fortunately, those who harbor this view are mistaken. It would be very unfortunate, indeed, if sophistry could not be avoided, for then no honest or morally scrupulous person could, in good conscience, have anything to do with the process of persuasion. Yet most of us find ourselves inclined or obliged to try to persuade others to act or feel in ways we think desirable and honorable. Rare is the person who can completely bypass the business of persuasion. Most of us, in our daily contacts, are involved in it most of the time.

There are some skills that can be used for good or evil purposes. They can be used scrupulously, in good conscience, or unscrupulously. The skill of the physician or surgeon can be used to cure or maim; the skill of the lawyer, to promote justice or to defeat it; the skill of the technologist, to construct or destroy. The skill of the persuader—the political orator, the commercial salesman, the advertiser, the propagandist—can be used with a high regard for truth and to achieve benign results, but it can also be as powerfully employed to deceive and injure.

Sophistry is always a misuse of the skills of rhetoric, always an unscrupulous effort to succeed in persuading by any means, fair or foul. The line that Plato drew to distinguish the sophist from the philosopher, both equally skilled in argument, put the philosopher on the side of those who, devoted to the truth, would not misuse logic or rhetoric to win an argument by means of deception, misrepresentation, or other trickery.

The sophist, in contrast, is always prepared to employ any means that will serve his purpose. The sophist is willing to make the worse appear the better reason and to deviate from the truth if that is necessary in order to succeed.

In ancient Greece, the sophists were teachers of rhetoric for the purpose of winning lawsuits. Each citizen who engaged in litigation had to act as his own lawyer—his own prosecutor or defense attorney. To those who regarded success in winning a lawsuit as an end that justified the use of any means, whether honorable or not, the sophistical misuse of rhetoric recommended itself.

That is how rhetoric first got a bad name, which it has never been able to shake off completely; it is important for all of us to remember that sophistry is an unscrupulous use of rhetoric. The thing misused is not itself to be condemned.

There can be honesty and dishonesty in selling, or in other efforts at persuasion, as in many other human transactions. A sales talk need not resort to lies and deceptions in order to be effective; nor need successful selling employ the devices of the con artist. What I have just said about selling applies to other forms of persuasion and other uses of rhetoric.

I am aware that, in certain quarters, these terms—salesmanship, persuasion, rhetoric—are terms of ill repute. But once it is understood that their connection with sophistry is adventitious, not inescapable, I see no reason for giving the terms up. They refer to activities in which all, or most, of us engage and can do so without recourse to reprehensible trickery, lies, or deception.

CHAPTER IV

The "Sales Talk" and Other Forms of Persuasive Speech

· I ·

The title of this chapter may arouse the reader's misgivings. What does a philosopher know about how to make a sales talk? That is hardly a subject which falls within his ken.

To set the reader's mind at rest on this score, I am going to start right out by doing what Aristotle, who was also a philosopher, recommended as the first step to be taken by anyone trying to persuade anyone else about anything, especially in the sphere of the practical.

Many years ago, when the Institute for Philosophical Research was established in San Francisco, an invitation came to me as its Director to address a luncheon meeting of the associated Advertising Clubs of California. They asked me in advance for a title. I suggested that it be "Aristotle on Salesmanship," a title I thought would be sufficiently shocking to them. It was. No one had ever before connected the name of Aristotle with salesmanship—or with advertising, which is an adjunct of selling.

The speech I delivered began by explaining the title. Advertising was a form of selling, was it not? I asked.

They nodded assent. And was not every form of selling an effort at persuasion, in this case an effort to persuade potential customers to buy the product advertised? Again they nodded.

Well, then, I went on, Aristotle is the master of that art—the art of persuasion—about which he wrote a lengthy treatise entitled "Rhetoric." To boil down its essential message for the occasion, I told them that Aristotle pointed out the three main tactics to be employed if one wished to succeed in the business of persuasion. There are no better names for these three main instruments of persuasion than the words the Greeks used for them: *ethos, pathos,* and *logos.* That, in a nutshell, is all there is to it.

Before I explain the tactics these three words name, I must report that the advertising experts assembled at that luncheon were so impressed by Aristotle's know-how about their own business that, as I learned afterwards, the bookstores of San Francisco were besieged that afternoon by members of the audience trying unsuccessfully to buy copies of Aristotle's *Rhetoric.*

The Greek word *ethos* signifies a person's character. Establishing one's character is the preliminary step in any attempt at persuasion. The persuader must try to portray himself as having a character that is fitting for the purpose at hand.

If, facing an audience of one or more persons on a particular occasion, you wish others to listen to you not only attentively but also with a sense that what you have to say is worth listening to, you must portray yourself as being the kind of person who knows what you are talking about and can be trusted for your honesty and good will. You must appear attractive and likeable to them as well as trustworthy.

To achieve this result with my audience of advertising specialists, I told them two stories about myself. The first was about a conversation I had had with one of Encyclopaedia Britannica's bankers at the time that that company was spending large sums of money on the production of *Great Books of the Western World* and the *Syntopicon*, of which I was editor.

The banker came to that meeting highly skeptical of the saleability of the product on which the company was spending so much money, and especially skeptical about this strange thing called the *Syntopicon* that threatened to consume more than a million dollars—a lot of money in those days—before it was completed. What good would the *Syntopicon* do anybody that might arouse their desire to purchase the set with the *Syntopicon* attached to it? "I, for example, am interested in buying and selling," the banker said; "and if I went to the *Syntopicon's* inventory of 102 great ideas, would I find one on salesmanship?"

That stumped me for a moment because, of course, the word "salesmanship" does not appear among the names of the 102 great ideas, nor does it even appear in the list of 1,800 subordinate terms that provide an alphabetical index referring to aspects of the 102 great ones. I got over being stumped by asking him a question.

Did he agree that to sell anybody anything one must know how to persuade them to buy what one wanted to sell? He agreed at once. I then clinched the matter by telling him that one of the 102 great ideas is rhetoric, which is concerned with persuasion, and that, if he consulted the *Syntopicon's* chapter on that idea, he would find many extremely helpful passages in that chapter, even though none of the great authors cited there ever used the word "salesmanship."

That was all I had to do to put an end to the banker's qualms about the money being spent on the production of the *Syntopicon*. I had sold him on it. I then told my audience in San Francisco the story of how I had to sell five hundred sets of *Great Books of the Western World* in order to raise enough money to defray the printing and binding costs for a first edition.

I did this almost single-handed, first by writing a letter that Bob Hutchins (who was then President of the University of Chicago) and I sent out over our signatures to 1,000 persons who might feel honored to become patrons of a special first edition of the set by purchasing it in advance of publication at the cost of $500—again a lot of money in the nineteen fifties.

That one letter brought in 250 purchase orders accompanied by checks. The 25 percent rate of return on a single appeal struck my audience of advertising men as an unparalleled success in the business of direct-mail advertising. I followed that initial success by selling the remaining 250 sets to individual patrons, either on the phone or by visiting them in their offices.

On one such occasion, I sold the head of a chain of over eighty department stores forty-five sets—one to be given away by each of the forty-five stores in its hometown to the local library or college as a public relations gesture. This particular sale took less than thirty minutes to make. The chief executive clearly indicated that he had little time to give me on a late Friday afternoon when he was about to leave town for the weekend. So I cut my sales talk to the bone in order to avoid impatience on his part, thereby gaining his good will.

By the time I had finished this second story, the advertising experts in my San Francisco audience were sufficiently impressed by my own personal involvement in the business of persuasion and of selling to be all ears when I then went on to explain how Aristotle had summed up the essence of salesmanship in his analysis of the three main factors in persuasion. I had succeeded in establishing my own *ethos* with them before I started to explain the role that *ethos*, *pathos*, and *logos* play in persuasion.

And that is what I hope I have just done with you by telling you these two stories about my own personal experience as an advertiser and a salesman.

· 2 ·

Of the three factors in persuasion—*ethos*, *pathos*, and *logos*—*ethos* always should come first. Unless you have established your credibility as a speaker and made yourself personally attractive to your listeners, you are not likely to sustain their attention, much less to persuade them to do what you wish. Only after they are persuaded to trust you, can they be persuaded by what you have to say about anything else.

There are, of course, many ways to take this initial step in the process of persuasion. You can do it by telling stories about yourself, the effectiveness of which will be heightened if they provoke laughter and the laughter is about you. You can do it more indirectly by underestimating your credentials to speak about the matter at hand, thus allowing the listeners to dismiss your underestimation as undue modesty. You can also do it by suggesting your association with others whom you praise for certain qualities that you hope your listeners will also attribute to you.

Two classic illustrations of the role of *ethos* in persuasion are to be found in the speeches made by Brutus and Marc Antony in Shakespeare's *Julius Caesar*. It is, of course, somewhat incongruous to refer to these two great orations as sales talks. They are instances of political persuasion, in which the attempt is to move the listeners to take one or another course of political action.

Nevertheless, practical persuasion is always selling, whether it be in the market place or in the political forum, across the counter or in a legislative chamber, in a commercial transaction or in a campaign for public office, in the advertisement of a product or in an appeal for a public cause or a political candidate.

In Shakespeare's play, you will remember, Julius Caesar has just been assassinated. The citizens of Rome, gathered near his dead body in the forum, grieving for their loss, angrily demand an accounting. Brutus, one of the conspirators who took part in the assassination, mounts the rostrum to address them:

Romans, countrymen, and lovers! hear me for my cause, and be silent, that you may hear: believe me for mine honour, and have respect to mine honour, that you may believe: censure me in your wisdom, and awake your senses, that you may the better judge. If there be any in this assembly, any dear friend of Caesar's, to him I say, that Brutus' love to Caesar was no less than his. If then that friend demand why Brutus rose against Caesar, this is my answer: Not that I loved Caesar less, but that I loved Rome more. Had you rather Caesar were living and die all slaves, than that Caesar were dead, to live all free men? As Caesar loved me, I weep for him; as he was fortunate, I rejoice at it; as he was valiant, I honour him: but, as he was ambitious, I slew him. There is tears for his love; joy for his fortune; honour for his valour; and death for his ambition. Who is here so base that would be a bondman? If any, speak; for him have I offended.

Who is here so rude that would not be a Roman? If any, speak;
for him have I offended. Who is here so vile that will not love
his country? If any, speak; for him have I offended. I pause for
a reply.

The citizens reply in unison: "None, Brutus, none."
Then, satisfied that he has persuaded them that the assassination was justified, Brutus yields his place to Marc Antony. Before Antony can speak, the populace, completely
won—or sold—by Brutus, shower him with acclaim and
proclaim the public honors they wish to bestow upon him
in dead Caesar's place. Brutus quiets them and implores
them to listen to Antony, to whom he has granted permis-
sion to speak. Thus introduced, Antony addresses them:

> Friends, Romans, countrymen, lend me your ears;
> I come to bury Caesar, not to praise him.
> The evil that men do lives after them;
> The good is oft interred with their bones;
> So let it be with Caesar. The noble Brutus
> Hath told you Caesar was ambitious;
> If it were so, it was a grievous fault,
> And grievously hath Caesar answer'd it.
> Here, under leave of Brutus and the rest—
> For Brutus is an honourable man;
> So are they all, all honourable men—
> Come I to speak in Caesar's funeral.
> He was my friend, faithful and just to me:
> But Brutus says he was ambitious;
> And Brutus is an honourable man.
> He hath brought many captives home to Rome,
> Whose ransoms did the general coffers fill:
> Did this in Casesar seem ambitious?
> When that the poor have cried, Caesar hath wept:
> Ambition should be made of sterner stuff:

> Yet Brutus says he was ambitious;
> And Brutus is an honourable man.
> You all did see that on the Lupercal
> I thrice presented him a kingly crown,
> Which he did thrice refuse: was this ambition?
> Yet Brutus says he was ambitious;
> And, sure, he is an honourable man.
> I speak not to disprove what Brutus spoke,
> But here I am to speak what I do know.
> You all did love him once, not without cause:
> What cause withholds you then to mourn for him?
> O judgement! thou art fled to brutish beasts,
> And men have lost their reason. Bear with me;
> My heart is in the coffin there with Caesar,
> And I must pause till it come back to me.

The short speech of Brutus mainly illustrates the role of *ethos*, as does the somewhat longer opening portion of Antony's address. Brutus, satisfied that he has exculpated himself and his fellow conspirators, does not try further to arouse the citizens to any course of action. He asks them only to allow him to depart alone. Antony, on the other hand, has a further purpose in mind. He wishes to avenge Caesar's death by arousing the multitude to take drastic action against the conspirators, especially Brutus and Cassius. (Honorable men, indeed!) To do this, he resorts to *pathos* and *logos*, the other two factors in persuasion.

· 3 ·

Whereas *ethos* consists in the establishment of the speaker's credibility and credentials, his respectable and admirable character, *pathos* consists in arousing the passions of the listeners, getting their emotions running in the direction of the action to be taken.

Pathos is the motivating factor. It makes its appearance fairly early in Antony's speech, commingled even in the opening passage with the development of the speaker's *ethos*. Antony reminds them of all the things that Caesar did for Rome, things from which they benefitted, and as he recounts these benefactions, he repeatedly asks them whether they can believe that Caesar displayed self-seeking ambition rather than dedication to the public good.

Antony thus succeeds in changing the mood that Brutus had established. One citizen cries out: "Caesar has had great wrong"; another exclaims: "He would not take the crown; therefore, 'tis certain he was not ambitious"; and still another expresses the admiration for Antony that Antony's use of *ethos* sought to produce, saying: "There's not a nobler man in Rome than Antony."

Satisfied now that he has established his own good character and also that he has their emotions running in the right direction, Antony proceeds to reinforce the passions aroused by adducing reasons for the action that he has sought to motivate.

Logos—the marshalling of reasons—comes last. Just as you cannot bring motivating passions into play, feelings in favor of the end result you are seeking to produce, until you have first aroused favorable feelings toward your own person, so there is little point in resorting to reasons and arguments until you have first established an emotional mood that is receptive of them.

Reasons and arguments may be used to reinforce the drive of the passions, but reasons and arguments will have no force at all unless your listeners are already disposed emotionally to move in the direction that your reasons and arguments try to justify.

How does Antony in the concluding portions of his ad-

dress commingle *pathos* and *logos* so effectively that he succeeds in moving the citizens of Rome to take arms against
Brutus, Cassius, and their associates?

First of all, in the course of other remarks he slyly gets
around to mentioning Caesar's will and intimating that,
when the citizens learn of its provisions, they will find
themselves Caesar's beneficiaries:

> O masters, if I were disposed to stir
> Your hearts and minds to mutiny and rage,
> I should do Brutus wrong, and Cassius wrong,
> Who, you all know, are honourable men:
> I will not do them wrong; I rather choose
> To wrong the dead, to wrong myself and you,
> Than I will wrong such honourable men.
> But here's a parchment with the seal of Caesar;
> I found it in his closet, 'tis his will:
> Let but the commons hear this testament—
> Which, pardon me, I do not mean to read—
> And they would go and kiss dead Caesar's wounds
> And dip their napkins in his sacred blood,
> Yea, beg a hair of him for memory,
> And, dying, mention it within their wills,
> Bequeathing it as a rich legacy
> Unto their issue.

The citizens beseech Antony to reveal the contents of
Caesar's will to them. But before he tells them that the
will provides a gift of seventy-five drachmas to every citizen, he launches into a peroration that raises their passions
to a fever pitch:

> If you have tears, prepare to shed them now.
> You all do know this mantle: I remember
> The first time ever Caesar put it on;
> 'Twas on a summer's evening, in his tent,

That day he overcame the Nervii:
Look, in this place ran Cassius' dagger through:
Through this the well-beloved Brutus stabb'd;
And as he pluck'd his cursed steel away,
Mark how the blood of Caesar follow'd it,
As rushing out of doors, to be resolved
If Brutus so unkindly knock'd or no;
For Brutus, as you know, was Caesar's angel:
Judge, O you gods, how dearly Caesar loved him!
This was the most unkindest cut of all;
For when the noble Caesar saw him stab,
Ingratitude, more strong than traitors' arms,
Quite vanquish'd him: then burst his mighty heart;
And, in his mantle muffling up his face,
Even at the base of Pompey's statue,
Which all the while ran blood, great Caesar fell.
O, what a fall was there, my countrymen!
Then I, and you, and all of us fell down,
Whilst bloody treason flourish'd over us.

This speech has the calculated effect. The citizens cry
out for revenge against the assassins and their cohorts,
calling them traitors and villains. They are no longer honorable men. But Antony, to be sure that he has won the
day and sold the populace of Rome the action he wishes
to be taken, takes one more step to consolidate his gains.
As the opening lines of his speech indicate, this action plays
once more on the *ethos* of Brutus as compared with the
ethos of Antony, epitomizes the reasons—the *logos*—for the
action to be taken, and confirms the feelings—the *pathos*—
he has already aroused:

Good friends, sweet friends, let me not stir you up
To such a sudden flood of mutiny.
They that have done this deed are honourable:

What private griefs they have, alas, I know not,
That made them do it: they are wise and honourable
And will, no doubt, with reasons answer you.
I come not, friends, to steal away your hearts:
I am no orator, as Brutus is;
But, as you know me all, a plain blunt man,
That love my friend; and that they know full well
That gave me public leave to speak of him:
For I have neither wit, nor words, nor worth,
Action, nor utterance, nor the power of speech,
To stir men's blood: I only speak right on;
I tell you that which you yourselves do know;
Show you sweet Caesar's wounds, poor poor dumb mouths,
And bid them speak for me: but were I Brutus,
And Brutus Antony, there were an Antony
Would ruffle up your spirits and put a tongue
In every wound of Caesar that should move
The stones of Rome to rise and mutiny.

"We'll mutiny!" the citizens roar. "We'll burn the house
of Brutus" and we'll go after the other conspirators. Then,
and only then, does Antony clinch the matter by revealing
how every citizen of Rome benefits from Caesar's will.
That does it. The citizens cry out "Go fetch fire. . . . Pluck
down the benches. . . . Pluck down forms, windows, anything." Satisfied that he has done the job, Antony retires,
saying to himself: "Now let it work. Mischief, thou art
afoot, take thou what course thou wilt!"

· 4 ·

To be effective in the use of *pathos*, in order to evoke
favorable emotional impulses, persuaders must bear two
things in mind.

First of all, they must recognize those human desires that they can depend upon as being present and actively motivating forces in almost all human beings—the desire for liberty, for justice, for peace, for pleasure, for worldly goods, for honor, good repute, position, or preference. Taking for granted that such desires generally abound with driving force, persuaders can call upon them for the objectives they have in mind, concentrating on the reasons why the course of action recommended is a better way of gratifying them than some alternative that a competitor might be trying to sell.

Here it is the *logos* rather than the *pathos* that persuaders must employ to tip the scales in their favor, whether they are trying to make their products more desirable than those of competitors or trying to make their candidate for public office preferable to an opponent for the office. Both products may serve the same purpose and so both may be responsive to a desire that exists and that they need only invigorate; their task, therefore, is to give the reasons why their product should be preferred.

Similarly, in political campaigning or in legislative debate about conflicting policies, where the emotional appeal is for the preservation of peace, the protection of liberties, or the securing of welfare benefits, persuaders do not have to create a desire for peace, liberty, or welfare. It is there to be used. They need only argue that their candidate or their policy serves that purpose better.

Persuaders cannot always count on desires that are generally prevalent in their audiences and ready to be brought into play. Sometimes they must instil the very desire that they seek to satisfy with their product, their policy, or their candidate. Sometimes people have needs or wants that are dormant, needs or wants of which they are not fully aware. These, persuaders must try to awaken and vitalize. Sometimes they must try to create a desire that is novel— generally inoperative until they have aroused it and made it a driving force. This is what must be done with a new product on the market. So, too, this is what a candidate for public office must do if his or her claim to it is based on a novel appeal.

The element of *ethos* may either precede or be combined with the employment of *pathos* in the sales talk. The role of the PR expert or the Madison Avenue consultant is to make the company that is trying to sell a product look good as well as to make the product itself more desirable than what the competition has to offer. When such experts in persuasion work for a political candidate, they work in the same way. They try to paint a glowing picture of their candidate's character in addition to activating the motives for subscribing to the policies for which he or she stands.

· 5 ·

With *ethos* and *pathos* fully operative, *logos* remains the winning trump in the persuader's hand. Here there are things to be avoided as well as things to be done well.

Above all, the persuader should avoid lengthy, involved, and intricate arguments. The task to be performed is not to produce the conviction that can result from a mathematical demonstration or scientific reasoning. Effective persuasion aims at much less than that—only a preference for one product, one candidate, or one policy over another. Hence the argument to be employed should be much skimpier, much more elliptical, much more condensed.

Persuaders must, therefore, omit many steps in the reasoning they present to catch the minds of their listeners. The classical name for such reasoning is the Greek word *enthymeme*, which signifies a process of reasoning with many premises omitted. The unmentioned premises must, of course, be generalizations that the persuader can safely assume will be generally shared. In arguments before a judicial tribunal, counsel for the prosecution or defense can take for granted certain generalizations of which the court takes judicial notice because, being generally acknowledged as true, they do not have to be explicitly asserted.

With such generalizations taken for granted, the persuader can go immediately from a particular instance, one that falls under the assumed and unmentioned generalization, to the conclusion that the applicable generalization entails. This is arguing from example. If I wish to persuade my listeners that a particular product or policy should be bought or adopted, I can do so effectively by showing how it exemplifies a generally accepted truth.

I do not have to assert that whatever contributes to a person's health is good. I need only describe my product as doing just that and doing it in full measure. I do not have to assert that everyone has a right to earn a living and that those who remain unemployed through no fault of their own suffer a serious injustice. I need only describe my policy as one that will increase employment. If I am prosecuting someone indicted for a serious crime, I do not have to assert that suddenly leaving the vicinity of the crime is an indication of guilt. I need only produce evidence to show that the prisoner at the bar did precisely that and that his departure has no other explanation.

Brevity or sparsity of reasoning is not the only factor in presenting a persuasive argument. Another is the employment of what are called rhetorical questions. Rhetorical questions are those so worded that one and only one answer can be generally expected from the audience you are addressing. In this sense, they are like the unmentioned premises in abbreviated reasoning, which can go unmentioned because they can be taken for granted as generally acknowledged.

Thus, for example, Brutus asks the citizens of Rome: "Who is here so base that would be a bondman?" adding at once: "If any, speak, for him have I offended." Again Brutus asks: "Who is here so vile that will not love his country?" Let him also speak, "for him I have offended." Brutus dares to ask these rhetorical questions, knowing full well that no one will answer his rhetorical questions in the wrong way.

So, too, Marc Antony, after describing how Caesar's conquests filled Rome's coffers, asks: "Did this in Caesar seem ambitious?" And after reminding the populace that Caesar thrice refused the crown that was offered him, Antony asks: "Was this ambition?" Both are rhetorical questions to which one and only one answer can be expected.

· 6 ·

In the course of explaining how the three essential elements in persuasion operate to make it effective, I have indicated the various kinds of speaking with a practical purpose that I have lumped together under the general heading of the sales talk. We normally restrict that term to obvious instances of salesmanship in the advertising and selling of commercial products. But speaking with a practical purpose in the political arena, in the legislative chamber, in a courtroom where someone is being prosecuted or defended, at a public ceremony where someone is to be honored or something is to be commemorated—all these, no less than winning customers for a product, involve selling.

Every form of public speaking with a practical purpose involves the same three essential factors in persuasion that must be employed in successful salesmanship. What has just been said applies equally to practical speaking that is not public—the kind of speech made by the chairman of the board to his colleagues, the kind of speech made by the proponent of a certain policy at a business conference, and even the kind of speech made by one member of a household to the rest of the family, with the practical purpose of getting them to adopt a recommendation being advanced.

In the classic expositions of practical rhetoric, from Aristotle, Cicero, and Quintilian down to the present, such terms as "selling" and "salesmanship" do not occur. The kinds of practical speaking are enumerated under such headings as *deliberative* (which refers to political oratory in legislative assemblies), *forensic* (which refers to the kind of speech that occurs in judicial proceedings, as, for example, counsel's summation to a jury), and *epidictic* (which refers to any effort to praise or dispraise something, whether that be a person or a policy), all of which are forms of persuasion.

It should be obvious that selling a product, like praising a person or a policy, is an effort at eulogistic persuasion. It should be no less obvious that political and forensic oratory are efforts to persuade the listeners to buy something—a policy being advocated or an evaluative judgment.

CHAPTER V

Lectures and Other Forms of Instructive Speech

· I ·

You can skip this chapter and the next if you never expect to be called upon to deliver a lecture. Or you may read these two chapters glancingly and with some sense of relief that you do not have to take the pains that others do in order to perform well in sustained speech to silent listeners.

However, if any business in which you are engaged or any aspect of your professional career ever threatens to demand such performance on your part, you may profit from the recommendations set forth in this chapter and the next. Much that I have to say about giving and preparing to give an academic lecture applies, in part at least, to shorter and less formal addresses or speeches.

Even if you are not by profession a teacher, as I am, and so are not called upon to give formal lectures, you may nevertheless, on one occasion or another, be obliged to speak at some length to an audience—at a business meeting, at a political rally, at a staff conference, to fellow club members, or even to fellow guests at a dinner party.

For your purposes on such occasions, my recommendations for preparing and delivering formal lectures may be too detailed and elaborate, but you can adapt them or cut them down to fit the circumstances, following them to the extent to which they are applicable.

I have already called attention to the fact that in the original meaning of the term "lecture," the lecturer was first of all a reader.

Today, though lecturing is still an oral or spoken presentation, lecturing is more closely associated with writing than with reading. Lectures are often written out before being delivered, either in full or in notes, and sometimes a written exposition is turned into a lecture for oral delivery. Nevertheless, the differences between the two forms of presentation—written and spoken—are such that the ability to write effectively does not always go hand in hand with the ability to speak effectively. In fact, the contrary occurs more often than not.

Both forms of presentation, written and spoken, consist in telling, and telling is always teaching, though there are other forms of teaching than by telling. When I tell you what I know, think, or understand and do so with the intention of instructing your mind, I am engaged in teaching you. Herein lies the essential difference between the sales talk, on the one hand, and the lecture and other forms of instructive speech, on the other.

There are many kinds of talk—baby talk in the nursery, small talk at dinner parties—but persuasive and instructive speech represent the two basic forms of speaking with which we shall be concerned. They are essentially different by virtue of the fact that the one aims at affecting the action or feelings of the listeners while the other aims at affecting their minds. Both involve persuasion, but for a different purpose.

It may be thought that lecturing as a form of teaching should aim to convince the mind rather than merely to persuade it. But conviction carries with it a degree of certitude that is seldom if ever attainable outside the sphere of mathematics and the exact sciences. An effective oral presentation that aims to convince the minds of its listeners of the truth of certain propositions need only have the order, clarity, and cogency that sound logic confers upon it. No rhetorical considerations enter. Here the differences between a written and an oral presentation of the same material become almost negligible.

We shall be concerned, therefore, mainly with the kind of speaking which aims to produce a more modest result—the persuasion of the mind, not beyond the shadow of a doubt, but beyond reasonable doubt, or simply by a preponderance of the evidence or of reasons in favor of one view rather than another. Here sound logic is not enough, and here we must be attentive to rhetorical considerations that arise from important differences between the spoken and the written presentation of the same material.

Just as the term "sales talk" can be used to cover all forms of *practical* persuasion—political oratory, ecclesiastical sermons, legal argument, business negotiations, ceremonial eulogies, as well as getting people to buy a product in the marketplace, so the term "lecture" can be used to cover all forms of instructive persuasion—efforts at persuasion that aim at an intellectual or theoretical rather than a practical result, a change of mind rather than a change of feeling or of impulse to act in one way rather than another.

Not quite all forms, because I have already excluded the kind of teaching, in mathematics or the exact sciences, that seeks to produce conviction concerning the truth of certain principles or conclusions. I would also exclude the kind of spoken presentation that aims only to convey a certain body of information to the listeners. To be effective, such presentations need only be grammatically correct and proceed at a pace that allows the listeners to absorb the details of information being presented. Effectiveness here does not depend either upon sound logic or upon skillful rhetoric.

Since the information thus imparted will be acquired mainly by the memory of the listeners, it can, in most cases, be imparted more effectively in writing than by speech. If speech is employed for any reason, it should be accompanied by a written document that can be read and reread. Memorization can thus be more readily ensured.

With these exclusions observed, what are we left with? First of all, the kind of lectures that occur in the classrooms of our educational institutions, the canonical fifty-minute talks that may take place with or without interruption by the listeners. Secondly, there is what, in distinction from the fifty-minute classroom talk, I call a formal lecture, delivered in a lecture hall to an audience of any size and always without interruption. The lecture hall may be located in an educational institution and the formal lecture may be intended only for listeners who are students in that institution, or it may be a public lecture hall and the audience be the public in general.

These two, though they are the two to which the word "lecture" is most commonly applied, are not the only forms of instructive speech. Sermons from the pulpit of a church or any religious congregation are also instances of teaching when they consist in commentary on a biblical text or an explanation of it, usually a passage from the lesson of the day. Sermons can, of course, be oratorical rather than didactic when they consist in practical persuasion, aiming to change the will or conduct of the listeners rather than trying to improve their understanding.

In addition to classroom talks, formal lectures, and didactic sermons, instructive speech also occurs in the world of business. A conference of business executives may be addressed by its chief executive or by one of its members for the purpose of imparting knowledge of the business at hand, for the purpose of analyzing a business problem to be solved so that it is better understood, or for the purpose of stimulating thought about the operation of the business.

Military staff meetings may also involve addresses by a military leader for one or another of the three purposes mentioned above in the realm of business conferences. The obvious differences between a classroom, a lecture hall, a church, a business conference, and a military staff meeting do not affect what is common to all these forms of lecturing, for they all involve telling that is instructive—speech that seeks to affect the minds of an audience by increasing what it knows, improving what it understands, or stimulating it to think in ways it has not thought before.

Anything more? Yes, instructive speech may even occur at a dinner table or in a drawing room when the host or hostess invites one of the guests, usually the guest of honor, to address those assembled on a topic concerning which the person asked to talk is thought to have some special competence or expertise.

With regard to all these diverse occasions when instructive speech occurs, I would like to restrict our attention for the moment to the kind of teaching by telling that consists in uninterrupted speech, with the listeners remaining silent until the oral presentation is completed.

I do so because I want to consider, in Part Three, what must be done by an audience that listens silently to a lecture or speech in order for that listening to be effective. I wish to reserve for Part Four the consideration of two-way talk—not only the kind of interchange between speaker and listener who are engaged in questioning and answering (which occurs in conversations of all sorts and in teaching by discussion), but also the kind of two-way talk that occurs when an instructive speaker of any sort stops speaking and invites questions from his or her listeners, whether that happens to occur in a classroom, in a lecture hall, in a business meeting, in a military staff conference, or in a private home.

What I have just said applies to sales talks as well as to lectures. The sales talk may proceed for a time—to be effective, for a short time—without interruption, but then it, too, should be immediately followed, first, by questions asked by the practical persuader, then by questions from others. When this happens, something like a conversation or discussion follows uninterrupted speech.

· 2 ·

For the same reason that listening is more difficult than reading, lecturing is more difficult than writing. The reason is that both listening and speaking, unlike writing and reading, take place in a limited span of time and occur in an irreversible flow. One can go back over what one has written or read. One can do so for any length of time, until one is satisfied that the writing or reading has been as well done as possible. The silent listener must catch on the fly what is being said. That imposes on the audience of a lecture the obligation to be persistently attentive. What is lost by flagging attention, or by turning the speaker off while one's mind turns to other things, is irretrievably lost.

So, too, the uninterrupted speaker must do whatever is necessary to sustain without break the attention of an audience. In the limited time allowed for a lecture or a speech, the speaker must so arrange the parts of the speech that listeners are able to follow easily what is being said and preserve it in their minds as they are moved from one point to another by the continuous flow of the speech.

Precisely because uninterrupted speech and silent listening are more difficult to do well than writing and reading, they are both rendered more effective when instructive speech is followed by two-way talk—by conversation or discussion, by questions and answers, by some kind of forum in which speaker and listener can engage in an active interchange.

If, for any reason, a speech must be presented without giving its listeners the opportunity for such active interchange with the speaker, the speaker would be well-advised to overcome the difficulties of listening by providing those whom he is trying to instruct with the substance of his remarks in some written form. Reading can then make up for the deficiencies in listening that are likely to occur and that are not remedied by discussion after the lecture is over.

When lecturing is not supplemented by a discussion that helps the speaker make sure that the minds of the listeners have been reached and moved, and when listening is not supplemented by reading in the absence of what can be accomplished by discussion, lecturing becomes the most ineffective form of teaching. It may amount to no more than the notes of the lecturer becoming the even more fragmentary notes of the listeners without passing through the minds of either. Only the memory may be affected, and it may be a very poor and even a distorted memory of what has been heard.

This happens most frequently in the fifty-minute talk by the classroom teacher. Remarkably different is the formal lecture that is the rule rather than the exception in European universities. Such lectures have been specially prepared for the occasion and are seldom, if ever, repeated over and over again as are the fifty-minute classroom talks by American teachers. The latter are seldom, if ever, worth transforming into written and publishable form. A series of formal lectures in the European style, which are the exception rather than the rule in American universities, usually do become the chapters of a published book after they have been delivered.

I cannot refrain here from telling the story of an invitation extended by the University of California to Professor Etienne Gilson of the College de France, one of its luminaries in the field of the history of ideas and a remarkable philosopher to boot. The invitation to become a visiting lecturer at Berkeley carried with it an honorarium that the French scholar found most alluring, so alluring that he was impelled to ask the authorities at the University of California what was expected of him, should he accept the invitation.

The reply informed him that he would be expected to deliver twelve lectures a week, the regular load of a teaching professor at the University. To M. Gilson this expectation called upon him to do what he regarded as absolutely impossible. He replied that, at the College de France, he never gave more than one lecture a week, and usually not more often than one every two weeks. It took him that amount of time to prepare a lecture.

How could anyone be expected to prepare twelve lectures in one week and do that week after week for the period of a semester? Absolutely impossible, Professor

Gilson said, declining the invitation and pointing out that when he finished delivering a series of such formal lectures, they were usually published in book form. Instead of inviting him to come to Berkeley, he suggested that it would be much less expensive for the University of California to buy his books and give them to the students to read.

· 3 ·

I said earlier that imparting information to an audience that desires the information in question involves neither logical nor rhetorical skill. One need only speak at a tempo and in a voice that enables the items of information to be heard clearly and distinctly. The details should be presented in an orderly fashion so that, if intrinsic connections exist, one item of information naturally leads to another.

Lectures that aim to give instruction in mathematics and the exact sciences must certainly be controlled by the inner logic of the subject, but the only rhetorical skill required to give such lectures effectively is making sure that the problem to be solved is understood before the solution is offered, and then being as clear as possible about the steps to be taken in reaching the solution. Here, too, the steps should be ordered so that one leads to another in a manner most cogent.

Of course, there is more to effective instruction even in the sphere of mathematics and the exact sciences. If laboratory demonstrations are involved, a certain amount of showmanship in setting them up and carrying them off contributes to the effect that is sought. Above all, intellectual excitement on the part of the teacher (even though what is being dealt with is old hat to the teller) serves to produce like excitement on the part of the listener. Without it, the telling, however logical and clear, remains a dull recitation that turns the audience off rather than on.

A good lecturer, in short, must have some of the gifts of a good actor. Each time the curtain goes up, no matter how many times it has gone up before for the lecturer, it should always seem like a new performance for the audience. Their sense of novelty should be heightened by the sense that the speaker is discovering for the first time the truths he is expounding. The skill of lecturers in dramatizing the moments of discovery will draw listeners into the activity of discovering the truths to be learned. Without such activity on their part, there can be little genuine learning. What results will be little more than a stuffing into a memory of matters soon to be forgotten.

What has just been said applies to all forms of instructive speech, but the role of rhetoric looms much larger when the speaker is not imparting information or expounding the truths of mathematics and the exact sciences. When we leave these two things behind, we come to speaking that aims to persuade the minds of listeners to adopt a certain view that has not been theirs before or to change from a view they have held to a view that is offered to replace it.

In all such efforts, the speaker must take into account the character of the audience being addressed. A lecture on a given subject with a given end result in view should not be given to any audience at random. I have often been invited to talk on a particular topic to an audience for whom, in my judgment, it would be inappropriate to speak on the subject chosen. One must have a certain degree of confidence that the subject selected is one that holds some initial interest for the audience to be addressed and that their general background will enable one to enlarge that interest.

More than such initial receptivity is required. The speaker should be able to make a fairly shrewd guess concerning the general character of the views about the subject chosen that are likely to be prevalent among the listeners. If they are in line with the views the speaker is going to present, the task is to confirm and reinforce them and, perhaps, expand them. That is much easier than to alter them and substitute contrary views for them.

To persuade listeners to change their minds by adopting views contrary to ones they have persistently and, perhaps, obstinately held, it is necessary to undermine their prejudices in a manner that is as firm as it is gentle.

Long-standing prejudices are barriers to persuasion. They must be removed before positive persuasion can begin. Removing them opens the mind and renders it receptive to views of a contrary tenor.

Thinking about the state of mind of the audience you are going to address and its relation to the subject about which you are going to speak is still not enough. You must also think about their state of mind in relation to your own person. Your listeners may harbor prejudices or suspicions about you that constitute obstacles to be overcome before positive persuasion can begin. Portraying your *ethos* in a favorable light plays a role in lecturing that is important to a degree only slightly less important than what is required by an effective sales talk.

If you cannot rely upon the fact that some favorable impression of your character and competence has been conveyed to your audience in advance of your speaking to them, you must do whatever is necessary to establish your authority to speak on the subject chosen.

It is, of course, better if someone else does this for you, either in a prior announcement of the event or while introducing you to the audience before you take over the rostrum, but it is never safe to rely too much on such preliminary portrayals of your *ethos*. In my experience, they are too often overdone or underdone, and you must make the necessary corrections to establish your character in a truer perspective.

I will never forget one occasion when a misimpression of my *ethos* was so violently contrary to my character that I was almost precluded from addressing the audience about the subject I had chosen.

Liam O'Flaherty had been scheduled to address a public audience in a suburb of Chicage on Irish life and letters. Overindulgence at a celebration on New Year's Eve prevented him from making the scheduled appearance on January 3rd, and at the last moment I was invited to take his place by the manager of the affair, on the understanding that I would talk about the state of American education.

The introduction that preceded my talk told the audience I was not Liam O'Flaherty and that the subject would be education, not Irish life and letters. So far, so good, but what neither I nor the chairman who introduced me counted on was the large number of people who came in late, after the lecture began, and had to take seats in the front rows that were the only ones then available. In the poorly lighted auditorium, their faces and eyes were the only ones distinctly visible to me. I became so disturbed by the look of bewilderment and disbelief on their faces that I had to stop the lecture, explain who I was, why I

was there, and what I was going to talk about, before I
could be reasonably comfortable about going on.

· 4 ·

In addition to bringing your *ethos* into play to win a
sympathetic ear, it is also necessary in giving a lecture, as
well as in making a sales talk, to employ the factor of *pathos* in a manner that heightens the effectiveness of your
persuasive effort. I have already indicated how this should
be done in lectures concerned with subjects in the fields of
mathematics and the exact sciences. There it is simply a
matter of dramatically conveying intellectual excitement on
the part of the speaker, in order to generate like excitement on the part of the listeners. More than that is required when the subject to be treated falls in other fields.

In speech that aims at practical persuasion, you should
try to arouse emotional responses in your listeners that are
favorable to the course of action you wish them to take—
not only arouse them, but get them flowing steadily in the
direction of the action you wish them to engage in. The
control of *pathos* operates differently in instructive speech
that has a theoretical, not a practical, aim.

Here it is your own emotions that you must, first of all,
bring into play. You must manifest, as plainly as possible,
your own emotional attachment to the views you are presenting. Indifference on your part is deadly. Unless the
views you hold and wish your audience to adopt are advanced by you with emotional fervor, you can hardly expect to engender a lively interest in them on the part of
your audience, even less a willingness to consider sharing
them with you.

That emotional fervor can be displayed in what you have

to say about the problem you are discussing, or about the ideas you are advancing to solve it, or about the solution you are proposing, or about all three. For effectiveness in persuasion, it is not enough to be clear, cogent, and coherent, however desirable all these qualities are. The thinking you have done privately and are now publicly articulating in your speech must have emotional force as well as intellectual power. The minds of your audience must be moved as well as instructed, and their emotions, stirred by your own, are needed to do the moving.

The more abstract your argument becomes, the more remote from everyday experience it tends to be, the more it may appear "academic" to your audience, the more it is necessary for you to overcome the difficulties your audience is likely to have in listening to and following what you have to say. How? Strangely enough, by being more rather than less overtly physical in the manner of your presentation.

By this I mean the amount of physical energy you put into your voice, in the stance of your body, and in the gestures that employ motions of your head, your body, and your arms. Somehow the manifest concreteness of your bodily involvement in what you have to say and the physical energy expanded in saying it compensates for the abstractness and the remoteness from life of the ideas you are expressing.

A schematic diagram, on a blackboard or otherwise displayed, helps in the same way. It is something to point to, something to make gestures at while you are talking. When such an aid is not available, you can make up for its absence by sketching a diagram in the air by the motion of your hands.

"Here on the left," you may say, "is one of the extreme

views that I regard as untenable. And here on the right," now gesturing in the opposite direction, "is an opposite extreme that is equally untenable. But in the middle, between them," and now your hands go up and down in the center, "is the moderate view that reconciles the half-truths contained in the two extremes." From that point on, you can keep your listeners thinking about the three views you are comparing and evaluating by pointing to the left, to the right, or to the center, as you speak.

A similar device is to use your fingers for calling attention to a succession of points that you wish your listeners to bear in mind. "Here is the first point," you will say raising your hand with one finger extended. "And here is the second point," accented by a similar gesture, now with two fingers extended; and so on.

Accompanying such physical gesturing, your tone of voice should be so modulated that it rises when a point of stress occurs, and falls when you are simply making a transition to another point of stress.

Most human beings, even those who have had sufficient schooling, find it difficult to rise above their imaginations or to think without appealing to vivid images and concrete examples. But abstractions—and often abstractions of a fairly high level—are indispensable to thinking about any important subject, certainly any subject that involves fundamental ideas.

Thinking about such subjects can seldom be done well entirely in concrete terms; what is worse, such thought is often distorted or confused by appeals to the imagination or to concrete examples that tend to obscure rather than clarify the ideas involved. It is, therefore, necessary to lift the minds of your listeners to levels of abstraction that exceed the reaches of their imaginations.

· 5 ·

From more than fifty years of delivering formal lectures, both in universities and to public audiences of all sorts, I have learned one lesson that is relevant to the matters just considered. Never talk down to your audience about any subject. If you do so, they will quite rightly turn you off. Why should they make much effort to listen to you if you are telling them things they already know or fully understand?

Always risk talking over their heads! By the emotional fervor of your speech, by its physical energy and your manifest bodily involvement with materials that are obviously abstract, you should be able to get them to stretch their minds and reach up for insights they did not have before.

It will not hurt if some of the things you say may be beyond their reach. It is much better for them to have the sense that they have succeeded in getting some enlightenment by their effort to reach up (even if they also have the sense that some things to be understood have escaped them) than it is for them to sit there feeling insulted by the patronizing manner in which you have talked down to them.

The truly great books, I have repeatedly said, are the few books that are over everybody's head all of the time. That is why they are endlessly rereadable as instruments from which you can go on learning more and more on each rereading. What you come to understand each time is a step upward in the development of your mind; so also is your realization of what remains to be understood by further effort on your part.

So far as the enlargement of your understanding is concerned, any book that does this for you is, ipso facto, a great book *for you*, though it may not be one for others. What is true of books to be read is true of lectures to be listened to. The only lectures that are intellectually profitable for anyone to listen to are those that increase one's knowledge and enlarge one's understanding.

The policy that I so strongly recommend—pitching what you have to say over the heads of your audience—must be moderated by two cautions. One is to gauge accurately the level of your audience so that you do not so far exceed their grasp that there is nothing for them to hold on to in their effort to reach up.

With this in mind, the other caution is to be sure that there is enough that is well within their grasp so that what they can easily understand gives them a firm intellectual footing from which to stretch their minds. This will encourage them to make the effort. But stretch their minds you must if teaching by telling is to do any intellectual good at all.

As *ethos* and *pathos* play their respective parts in both the sales talk and the lecture, so does *logos*, here also with a difference. Whereas the arguments involved in selling, or in any other form of practical persuasion, should always be as abbreviated and as elliptical as possible, often to the point of being barely detectible, the logical content of a good lecture or an instructive speech should consist in arguments of extended length and fully explicit about the steps to be taken. The *logos* should be spelled out in detail.

Repetitions should be employed rather than avoided. They can be made more effective by reiterating the same point in a number of different ways. If an argument is elaborate and extended, as it often must be, it should be followed by a compact summary—boiled down to a statement of its message in a few brief and striking sentences. *Here it is in a nutshell.*

· 6 ·

Two other Greek words name additional considerations that apply to both instructive and persuasive speech. One is *taxis*; the other, *lexis*.

Taxis concerns the organization of a speech—the order of its three component parts. The first of these is its proem, its opening or introduction; the second, the main body of the speech; and the third, its peroration, its closing or conclusion.

In most sales talks, the opening should attempt to establish the speaker's *ethos* first. That should be followed by bringing *pathos* into play. *Logos* should be left until the end.

A sales talk, especially if it is conveniently short, has a relatively simple structure. A sales talk that is too complex in its organization and unduly extended in length will defeat its purpose. Many political orators make this mistake. Some of the greatest orations ever delivered are marvellous to read, but were almost impossible to listen to when given. Lincoln's Gettysburg Address is a justly celebrated exception.

A speech that is to be delivered to an audience that comes to listen for the sake of learning can have greater length and more complex organization. Its introductory portion should briefly sketch the whole—set forth the three or four main sections that constitute the structure of the speech—so that the audience is advised in advance of what they can expect to hear. Giving them such expectations enables them to listen more carefully and to follow closely what they are listening to. Their having from the outset a kind of map or chart of the journey to be taken through the speech makes it possible for them to detect, from time to time, what stage has been reached in the forward, ongoing flow of the speech.

The proem, or introduction to a lecture, should accomplish one other thing. The language in which it is couched and the way in which it is spoken should ensure getting the listeners' attention. Few speakers can avoid hemming and hawing here and there; few can avoid dropping an uncompleted sentence now and then; but at the very beginning, the speaker must not stumble in the least.

In those opening moments, what the speaker has to say should be said loud and clear, in simple forceful sentences, and without any hesitation or backtracking. Not only will such speaking get the attention desired, it will also set the tone and pace for the rest of the speech.

The main body of the speech should be arranged—its successive parts ordered and related—in the precise manner described in the speaker's opening remarks. The listeners were told then what the speaker planned to tell them, in what order the telling would take place, and how one thing would lead to another. The execution of the plan outlined at the beginning should make the speaker's own following of that outline as plain and manifest as possible.

If the main body of the speech consists, let us say, of three main parts, each should conclude with some summary of what has been said and should include a transition to what is coming next. Repetitions may be necessary to help the listeners discern where they have been, where they now are, and what they are about to move on to.

The reason why repetitions should be avoided in writing (because readers can turn back to earlier pages to refresh their memory of a point merely referred to and not spelled out once again) does not apply to speaking. On the contrary, repetitions are needed precisely because the listener cannot turn back to something said earlier and hear it all over again. The speech is continually moving forward, and the speaker must repeat something said earlier if the listener needs to have it in mind in order to understand a point being made later.

The peroration, or closing portion, of the lecture should be brief. If it is prolix, it defeats itself. It should manage to provide a summation of the whole in the shortest possible scope and with the maximum clarity. The closing sentences, like the opening ones, should be carefully constructed and eloquently delivered. They should be spoken slowly and in a tone of voice that conveys to the listeners the assurance that what has been said fulfills the promise made at the beginning concerning what was to be said. It should also carry some emotional manifestation of the speaker's sense of the importance to the listeners of what they have heard.

One word more about the length of a lecture. From thirty minutes to an hour is probably the most comfortable length for an audience. However, sometimes the substance to be covered requires a lecture to run longer than that. If that is the case, the speaker should find a breakpoint at which he can give the audience a short rest and then go on to the end.

I have found that if a lecture takes an hour and twenty minutes to deliver at a reasonable speed, it helps a great deal to announce in advance that you are going to pause briefly when you have finished the third major point after about fifty minutes have elapsed, and then go on with the remainder of the lecture in the next thirty minutes. At the break-point, you might even ask the audience to stand up in place, breath in and out three times and stretch, then sit right down so that you can go on with the speech.

The final consideration is *lexis*. Here we are concerned with the language or literary style of the lecture—the choice of words, the avoidance of ambiguity, or, if ambiguity is unavoidable in the use of certain words, calling attention to it by distinguishing the two or three different but related meanings with which a given word is being used.

So far as possible, the speaker's vocabulary should be designed so that it is generally consonant with the vocabulary of the audience. Generally, but not always, for it may be necessary for the speaker to introduce a number of terms that do not occur in the vocabulary of everyday speech.

These should be kept to the minimum, and when words that will appear strange or out of the ordinary to the audience are used, special attention should be called to them and their meanings carefully explicated.

Sometimes the lecturer must employ a term in common use in a sense that is far from common, and may even have a significance, as used in the lecture, that departs radically from its everyday meaning. Listeners will be confused unless great care is taken to make them aware of how a word of this sort is being used by the lecturer, and they may have to be reminded of it several times.

Keeping technical terms or terms of art to the minimum, and using common words with uncommon senses as infrequently as possible is, perhaps, the first rule of linguistic style in effective teaching by telling, especially in speaking to popular audiences. Jargon and esoteric language should be avoided at all costs.

The other rule of style can be stated in two sentences.

On the one hand, the language employed and the sentences constructed should be clear without being plain. On the other hand, they should have a certain elevation above the ordinary without being obscure. These rules are easy to state but very hard to follow.

CHAPTER VI

Preparing and Delivering a Speech

· I ·

The only speech for which no preparation is possible is the one you may be unexpectedly called upon to deliver by the toastmaster at a dinner party. Then you have to rely upon your wits—and wit. The saving grace on such occasions is that you can be sure that brevity will be appreciated and that wit rather than wisdom is expected from you. The substance of your remarks can be slight so long as their relevance is pointed.

Some speakers have confidence in their ability to speak extempore on other occasions when they know well in advance the character of the audience to be addressed and the subject they are called upon to cover. Except for the rare genius who can deliver an address that is solid in substance, perfect in form, and brilliant in its rhetorical devices, without notes of any sort, the rest of us would be well advised to do the work of careful preparation.

I have known a few such geniuses—Barbara Ward, for one, Adlai Stevenson, for another, and Mark Van Doren also. Their power of spontaneous utterance was such that eloquent sentences and well-rounded paragraphs flowed from their lips as readily as concertos and symphonies flowed from the pen of the youthful Mozart. I do not know what mental preparation they made before speaking, or how they formed the speech in their minds before delivering it. How they did it is not the point anyway, for geniuses of this variety do not need any help from what I have to say in this chapter.

Winston Churchill gave many the impression that he was a speaker of the same sort. Hearing him on radio during the opening days of the Second World War, I listened with awe at what appeared to be a beautifully organized speech, eloquently delivered with all the hesitations and pauses that indicated improvisation on his part. There were many moments when he appeared to be reaching for the right word to come next. But the truth of the matter was, as I later learned, that the speech was completely written out and delivered so cunningly that it had all the qualities of impromptu utterance.

How to achieve precisely that effect is the main objective of the recommendations I am going to make in this chapter. The suggestions that I have in mind will not turn anyone who follows them into a Churchill, for he, too, was a genius in his own way. However, my suggestions will, I think, enable anyone to achieve a modicum of Churchill's effect in delivering a speech.

Since all my recommendations call upon you to prepare for speaking by writing out, in some form, what you wish to say, it is, first of all, of great importance to recognize that what is written to be read has a radically different character from what is written to be heard. The remarkable difference between listening and reading—the one requiring you to keep moving forward irreversibly with the flow of the speech, the other allowing you to proceed at your own pace and to go forward or backward at will by simply turning the pages—demands that you accommodate what you write for listening, as contrasted with what you must do for readers.

The writer of an essay or a book to be published must, of course, have some image of his readers in mind, but that can seldom be as definite as the vision of an audience that the speaker expects to confront face to face. In addition, the written word to be read is unaccompanied by bodily gestures, facial expressions, modulations of voice, differential pauses, and all the other subtle paraphernalia of eloquent oral delivery. Hence, when you write for readers you must achieve whatever effects you seek to obtain by other means, whereas when you write speeches to be listened to you can and should so compose your utterances that you can anticipate in advance how the words you are going to speak will gain their effect by the nonverbal aspects of your delivery of them.

Except for the geniuses already mentioned, the advantages to the rest of us of preparing a speech by writing out notes for it should be quickly recognized. An essay or a book can be of any length because its readers are not compelled to take it in all at one sitting. Spoken utterance must always run for a limited time. You may know in advance that your remarks should take a half hour or less. Sometimes you may be advised that you can speak at greater length than that. In either case, you must do what is necessary to hold the audience's attention.

Hitler, Mussolini, and Stalin may have greatly exceeded the normal span of time for rapt listening, but they, being who they were, had captive audiences. Edmund Burke, too, delivered his great addresses to Parliament at much greater length than an hour, but the historic fact to remember is that when Burke rose to address the House, its members, almost to a man, filed out. His orations, intended for listeners, ended up being only for readers; perhaps he knew that that would be the case and planned for it.

· 2 ·

Once again, let us consider the task that confronts the rest of us who are not, for one reason or another, exceptions to the rule.

We have a half hour or an hour in which to catch and hold the attention of our listeners and, succeeding in that, to take advantage of it by getting across to them, in good order, the substance of what we have to say. Woe to the ordinary speaker who presumes that he can successfully disregard time limitations. I know this from a sad, and also funny, experience of my own.

When, in 1937, during the first year of the New Program at St. John's College at Annapolis, Maryland, I travelled there from the University of Chicago to deliver ten lectures on the philosophy of Aristotle to students who were engaged in reading the great books, I made the mistake of thinking that their interest in the subject must necessarily be so great that I could afford to lecture at whatever length might be necessary to cover the subject of each lecture. The lectures, completely written out for delivery, took me two hours or more to deliver, speaking at an unusually rapid rate.

The poor students suffered silently through it all, supposing that the ordeal they were experiencing was one of the novelties expected of them by the program in which they had voluntarily enlisted. It eventually dawned on them that this was not the case and that they were not expected to suffer such enormities. When I returned the next year to deliver another series of lectures, they devised ways of bringing me to a halt at the end of an hour.

On the occasion of my first lecture in 1938, at 9:15 P.M. on the button, one hour after I had started, all the alarm clocks owned by the students and hidden in the gallery of the lecture hall exploded in unison. I waited until they rang themselves out and finished the lecture.

At 9:15 P.M. on the second occasion, a student pulled the main switch to black out the lecture hall. I lit matches at the podium to see my notes and completed the lecture.

I finally did get the message and cut my lectures down to a listenable length. Ever since 1938, my annual lecture at St. John's College has not only been fashioned for delivery in an hour, more or less, but it has always been accompanied by a wittily concocted student prank that I enjoy as much as they do—a kind of memorial to a lecturer's mistake, which his listeners succeeded in correcting.

Given the limited span of time that no speaker should ever dare to exceed, the reason for making notes in advance should be clear. Without such preparation, one is bound to ramble and, especially if one is full of one's subject, even to go on at greater length almost involuntarily. By "rambling," I mean indulging in digressions at one point or another, giving more time to this point or that than is their due and would be accorded them in a well-planned speech.

To fit all the parts of one's speech into the allotted time and to fit them together in proper proportion to another, it is necessary to plot the organization of a lecture carefully and to have that plot written out and visibly present on the lectern as one speaks, just as most conductors of symphony orchestras turn the pages of the composer's score that they have in front of them on the podium. The conductors who perform without a score are, after all, not usually its composer, but only executive musicians who have remarkable gifts of memory. The lecturer, in contrast, is the composer of the speech as well as its executant.

If you are persuaded of the need to make notes for the delivery of a speech or lecture, you have a choice between two forms that these notes can take. They can either take the form of a skeletal outline of what is to be said, written in topical phrases, not in full sentences or paragraphs, or they can consist in the speech fully written out in prose paragraphs and thus looking exactly like an essay ready for publication.

At the meetings of learned societies or academic associations, the speeches delivered by scholars usually take the latter form. The speaker knows in advance that he is expected to submit his speech, as delivered, for subsequent publication in the proceedings of the conference. Anyone who has attended such meetings knows how deadly such lectures or speeches are, and few if any of those present listen with much attention, knowing that if the substance is worth paying attention to, they can read it with greater profit later. The speech that is read from a fully written out essay is almost impossible to listen to and seldom, if ever, deserves the monumental effort required to do so with sustained attention.

At the opposite extreme is the other form of written preparation, the brief skeletal outline in topical phrasing, the briefer, the more skeletal and topical, the better. When I first delivered a speech to alumni of the University of Chicago on how to read a book, I did so from notes written on two sides of a single three-by-five card. With those notes before me, I managed to cover in an hour what later became a fully written out treatment of the subject in a book of over 300 pages.

Why, then, do I not recommend always adopting this skeletal and topical form of note-making for a lecture? My answer is that it works well only for certain subjects—subjects in which the speaker is in full command of all the elements that enter into an orderly treatment of the subject. In addition, it works well only if, from frequent speaking about that subject, the speaker's mind is saturated with all the words, phrases, and sentences needed for a clear, orderly, and cogent utterance of his or her thought about it.

If, on the contrary, the preparation of a lecture or speech to be delivered involves the speaker in original thinking about the subject selected for the occasion; if that thinking requires the speaker to formulate, for the first time, in appropriate language the thoughts that are forming in his mind for the first time; and if the speaker does not possess, as few of us do, the magnitude of memory needed to recollect that language effectively, without stumbling and bumbling when it is recalled by a page or two of skeletal, topical notes, then he or she had better have something more on the lectern than a brief topical outline in skeletal form.

· 3 ·

These things being so, must the speaker return to the opposite extreme that I have dismissed as deadly dull—the fully written out speech that the lecturer reads out loud to an audience and that would be much better read silently by them? Is there a middle ground between the two extremes? I think there is, and it is the one that Churchill employed when he spoke so effectively, as if he were improvising a speech that was completely written out.

The middle ground consists in the writing down of full sentences, either single sentences or several sentences together, in outline form arranged on the page by appropriate spacing, subordinations, and indentations. The look of such a page is quite different from a page that is covered by a succession of lengthy prose paragraphs. Because of the spacing, the subordinations, and the indentations of an outline, and especially because each line that is written down is short, with wide margins on both sides, so that it can be seen with a single glance of the eye, you can lift your eyes from the page and appear to be speaking without notes, or at least with only skeletal notes in front of you.

When a speech is written out in full the other way, in a succession of long paragraphs, there is simply no way of delivering it without plainly appearing to be reading from a manuscript, with all the disaffecting consequences that attend such a performance. Should you look up from the page in front of you in order to look at the audience as you read, you are likely to lose your place and stumble until you regain it.

The middle ground that I am recommending—the fully written out speech that is written down in outline form, with each unit of the outline a single sentence or two—enables you to avoid the appearance of reading and also to have complete control over what you are saying for the first time. It also assures you of accurate timing, for you can tell from past experience how many of such outlined pages will take an hour or so to deliver, and thus you will be able to avoid exceeding the allotted time. In addition, before speaking, you can make an accurate allotment of portions of the whole time to the successive parts of your speech, thus preventing digressions or excursions on this or that point, which may use up too much time, so that too little time is left for matters that deserve more.

· 4 ·

My description so far of the middle ground between the brief topical outline in skeletal form and the fully written essay that can only be read may not suffice to convey concretely what I have in mind. The only way to remedy this is to include in this book one clear example of the device I am recommending.

It is added as Appendix I. There you will find an address that I gave last year to the American Association of Neurological Surgeons at their annual meeting.

I had been invited by them to deliver what they called the Harvey Cushing Memorial Oration. I selected as my subject one that I thought appropriate for the occasion, the relation of minds to brains, considering angels, humans, and brutes, and also machines that are regarded as embodiments of artificial intelligence.

Though I had previously written books that had an intimate bearing on the subject—one some years ago, *The Difference of Man and the Difference It Makes*, and one very recently, *The Angels and Us*—the special occasion and the special audience impelled me to rethink what I wanted to say and to reformulate my thinking in language that would convey it effectively.

I therefore employed what I have called the middle ground between the two extremes of written preparation for delivering a lecture. I wrote what I wanted to say in full sentences, but I put them on paper in outline form, so that I could speak those sentences without appearing to be reading an essay. Turn to Appendix I and you will see how this is done and why it works in the way I have described.

The outlined lecture you will find in Appendix I may be instructive in other ways. It will exemplify, I think, many of the points that I made in the preceding chapter concerning the role that is played by the five factors or elements that enter into the construction of a lecture that tries to be persuasive as well as instructive, and listenable to boot—the factors or elements for which I have used the five Greek words *ethos, pathos, logos, taxis,* and *lexis.* They are there for you to find in my Harvey Cushing Memorial Oration. What you will miss, of course, are the bodily gestures, the facial expressions, the modulations of voice, and the pauses that accompanied the oral delivery of the speech you can read.

· 5 ·

I have not mentioned so far the early stages of preparing to write a speech in this outline form. My own initial steps of preparation are as follows. First of all, I refresh my memory of my earlier thinking on the subject, to be found in this case in books or essays already written and published. I then take a large yellow pad and, under the heading "Random Notes," put down whatever new thoughts come into my mind in whatever sequence they occur, almost like that of free association. I may cover many pages with such random notes.

My next step is to examine these notes and decide which

points are related to one another and how they are related to form a major unit of the speech. With this in mind, I then put down on paper a brief skeletal outline of the speech in topical form, indicating what should be covered in the introduction, what should constitute the three or four major sections of the speech, and what should be left for the peroration or conclusion.

That done, I am then ready to write the speech out in full, in the outline form exemplified in Appendix I. When that is neatly typed for me to read, I may revise it once or twice before delivering it, and often the experience of delivering it leads me to revise it once again before putting it in my file for possible use on other occasions for which it may be appropriate.

It always amazes me what one can learn from delivering a speech, things one cannot discover in advance of that experience. The reaction you get from your audience tells you something about how to improve your speech. Certain discomfort you experience in the actual delivery of the speech calls your attention to things you must change in order to make the speech more comfortable to deliver.

Audience reaction is an essential ingredient in this whole business of speaking. What you see on the faces or in the eyes of your listeners tells you almost instantaneously whether you are getting across, and what other effects are occurring. Such feedback is indispensable to effective speaking.

That is why it is always wise to insist upon the kind of lighting that enables you to see your listeners clearly. Auditoriums are sometimes lit in such a way that the speaker is in the spotlight and the audience in the dark. You might just as well be speaking to an empty hall if you cannot see, and even feel, through a speaker's antennae, what is going on in the minds of your listeners.

There are other cautions that a speaker should learn to bear in mind when inspecting the room in which he is going to speak. Will it be properly lighted? Is there a lectern or podium of the right height and with sufficient light on it to see one's notes? Does the amplifying sound equipment work, without wheezes or other noises? What are the acoustical properties of the hall that should control the decibel level of your speech?

Whenever possible, all these thing should be looked into in advance. To discover at the last moment that the physical conditions you need have not been adequately provided may be too late to remedy the defects.

· 6 ·

One other caution should be borne in mind. Speakers are sometimes invited to dinner parties before they address an audience. They are sometimes expected to meet the press for interviews about the lecture before it is given. In one way or another, the speaker may be drawn into giving his speech before he is scheduled to give it. These are serious drawbacks to be avoided like the plague.

One should obstinately refuse to speak about the subject selected for the occasion until one is on the platform, at the podium, and ready to go. If you cannot avoid engaging in conversation on other subjects in the hour before the lecture, the least you can do is to insist upon ten or fifteen minutes of solitude and silence before the curtain goes up. That may serve to restore the intellectual and vocal energy you need for the performance soon to begin.

In responding to invitations that inquired about the fee he expected to be paid for speaking, Mark Twain used to reply, in his preinflationary epoch, that he wanted $250 for speaking, but that the price was double if he was expected to come to dinner before he spoke.

Much of what I have said about speaking to a live audience face to face applies also to speaking to a live audience that is watching a television screen and even to taping a speech that will be telecast later. The use of a teleprompter replaces the notes on the lectern. When that instrument is skillfully used so that its use is unnoticeable to the viewers, the utterance sounds as if it were impromptu and unrehearsed, which is so attractive to listeners.

The speaker on television, whether in a live telecast or a taped one, has one advantage not available to the speaker in a lecture hall. By looking directly into the camera, he or she will be looking directly into the eyes of each person watching the television screen. When someone looks you directly in the eye, that tends to hold your attention. It is impolite to turn your eyes away.

In a lecture hall or auditorium, however well-lighted it may be, the speaker cannot look directly into the eyes of everyone present. You may focus on one person or on a small group, but your gaze must rove around the hall, as you speak, and so members of the audience can turn their gaze away from you when you are not looking directly at them.

There also is one great disadvantage to delivering a speech over television. You do so blind. You know the viewers are out there, but you cannot see their faces, you cannot feel their presence, you cannot discern the bodily movements or facial expressions that betray their inattention or reveal their rapt concentration. Speaking to an audience from which you get no feedback of this sort is, therefore, very much more difficult than speaking to listeners face to face.

PART THREE
Silent Listening

CHAPTER VII

With the Mind's Ear

Everyone, when they are young, has a little bit of genius; that is, they really do listen. They can listen and talk at the same time. Then they grow a little older and many of them get tired and listen less and less. But some, a very few, continue to listen. And finally they get very old and they do not listen anymore. That is very sad; let us not talk about it.

Gertrude Stein, as
reported by Thornton
Wilder

The ears have nothing comparable to eyelids, but they can be as effectively sealed as eyelids can be closed. Sometimes both close at the same time, but it is often the case that the ear is turned off while the eyes are open. That matters little if, in either case, the mind's attention is turned to other matters than what is being heard or seen. What the senses register are then sounds and sights that lack significance.

Listening, like reading, is primarily an activity of the mind, not of the ear or the eye. When the mind is not actively involved in the process, it should be called hearing, not listening; seeing, not reading.

The most prevalent mistake that people make about both listening and reading is to regard them as passively receiving rather than as actively participating. They do not make this mistake about writing and speaking. They recognize that writing and speaking are activities that involve expenditures of energy, unflagging attention, and the effort to reach out to the minds of others by written or oral communication. They also realize that some persons are more skilled in these activities than others and that increased skill in their performance can be acquired by attention to rules of art and by putting the rules into practice so that skilled performance becomes habitual.

As I pointed out in *How to Read a Book*, the first lesson to be learned about reading is that reading—with the mind, not just with the eye—must be every bit as active as writing. Passive reading, which is almost always with the eyes in motion but with the mind not engaged, is not reading at all.

That kind of reading is on a level with watching television for the sake of relaxation or just to fill some empty time, letting the images that pass across the screen flit before one's eyes. The habit of watching television in this way, endemic among the young who spend hours before the screen in a state of intellectual somnolence, turns them into passive readers who flip the pages of a book with little or no attention to the meaning of the words on the page or to the structure and direction of the discourse that the book contains.

Let me repeat an analogy that I have used before. The catcher behind the plate is just as active a baseball player as the pitcher on the mound. The same is true in football of the end who receives the forward pass and the back who throws it. Receiving the ball in both cases requires actively reaching out to complete the play. Catching is as much an activity as throwing and requires as much skill, though it is skill of a different kind. Without the complementary efforts of both players, properly attuned to each other, the play cannot be completed.

Communication through the use of words is comparable. It does not occur unless the reader's or listener's mind reaches out to catch what is in the mind of the writer or speaker. This has been directed to the reader or listener through the medium of written or spoken words. If we use only our eyes or ears to take in the words, but do not use our minds to penetrate through them to the mind that delivered them, we do not perform the activity that is essential to either reading or listening. The result is failure of communication, a total loss, a waste of time.

Of course, the fault may not always lie with the reader or listener. The failure to catch a wild pitch is not the catcher's fault. So, too, some pieces of writing and some spoken utterances are either so devoid of meaning and coherence or so befuddled and confusing in their use of words that the best reader and listener can make little sense of them. Some are such defective presentations of what is in the mind of the writer or speaker that they are not worth paying much attention to, if any at all.

In considering the effort and the skill required for active and effective listening, I am going to assume that the spoken utterance deserves close attention and will repay all the effort one can exert and all the skill at one's disposal to follow what has been said, so as to understand it to a degree that approximates the understanding that the speaker wishes to achieve.

For the moment, we can ignore the differences between the sales talk and the lecture, the differences in purpose and in style. We shall subsequently consider how, in the one case, listeners must be on guard against the tricks of persuasion that may occur in the effort to sell them something, to enlist their support for a political policy or candidate, or to get them to carry out a managerial decision to do business in a certain way. Similarly, in the other case, we shall subsequently consider how listeners must be both docile and critical, both predisposed to learn rather than resistant or indifferent to what is being taught, yet at the same time not wishing to swallow whole what is laid before them.

· 2 ·

The importance of listening is generally acknowledged. It is also generally recognized that, of the four operations involved in communication through words—writing, reading, speaking, and listening—the last of these is rarely well performed.

No one who gives a moment's thought to the matter would hesitate to confess that whatever degree of skill he has acquired in writing, reading, and speaking, he has acquired less—if any at all—in listening. If asked why this is so, one response may be that instruction in writing played a part in his schooling and that some attention, though much less (to a degree that is both striking and shocking) was paid to developing the skills of reading and speaking. Almost no attention at all was given to skill in listening.

Another response may be forthcoming from the person who reveals the mistaken impression that listening involves little more than keeping quiet while the other person talks. Good manners may be required, but not much skill.

We are all indebted to Sperry, a major American corporation, for the campaign it has conducted, both in the advertisements it has published and in the brochures it has distributed, to counteract the widespread apathy and misunderstanding that exists concerning listening. Sperry has also devoted corporate time and funds to developing courses of instruction in listening and has made these courses available to all levels of its personnel, because, in Sperry's view, deficiencies in listening and the failures of communication that ensue from such deficiencies are a major source of wasted time, ineffective operation, miscarried plans, and frustrated decisions in every phase of the businesses in which the corporation is engaged.

In one of Sperry's brochures, it is pointed out that of the four basic activities involved in communication, listening is learned first in the development of the child, used most in the course of one's life (46 percent of the time), and is the least taught throughout all the years of schooling.

In contrast, speaking is learned next in the developmental sequence, used 30 percent of the time, and is almost as untaught in school as listening is. Reading is learned before writing; it is engaged in more frequently than writing (15 percent of the time as compared to 9 percent); and less instruction is devoted to it than to writing.

Whether these facts and figures as presented can go unquestioned, it is certainly the case that the skills of speaking and listening are much less well developed in the population at large than those of writing and reading. However poor is the performance of our average high school and college graduates in writing and reading (and it would be difficult to exaggerate the inadequacy of their skills in these fundamental activities), it is many times worse with regard to speaking, and listening is certainly the worst of all.

The Sperry brochure to which I have been referring lists a number of bad habits that interfere with or detract from effective listening. Among them are paying more attention to the speaker's mannerisms of speech than to the substance of what is being said; giving the appearance of paying attention to the speaker while allowing one's mind to wander off to other things; allowing all sorts of distractions to divert one's attention from the speaker and the speech; overreacting to certain words or phrases that happen to arouse adverse emotional responses, so that one is then predisposed to be negative in one's prejudgment about what the speaker is actually saying; allowing an initial lack of interest in the subject to prevent one's hearing the speaker's explanation of why it is important and should be of interest; and, worst of all, taking an occasion for listening as nothing more than an occasion for indulging in daydreaming, and so not listening at all.

To overcome these bad habits, which all of us have detected in others if not in ourselves, the Sperry brochure then lists "ten keys to effective listening." Many of these recommendations are little more than injunctions to overcome or eliminate the bad habits already mentioned that stand in the way of effective listening.

Of the few recommendations that are positive, all concern the use of one's mind in listening. That, of course, is the nub of the matter. But it is not enough to say that one's mind must be actively engaged in listening, that its perceptions must not be clouded by irrelevant emotions, that the mental effort expended must be equal to the task set by the difficulty or complexity of what the speaker is saying.

Nor is it enough to say that the listener must have at least the intellectual courtesy of initially assuming that what is being said is of sufficient interest and importance to be worthy of attention. The speaker may fail to confirm that assumption, but at the beginning he should be listened to with an open mind and an attentive one.

· 3 ·

What more can be said, and must be said, to provide positive rules that one can follow and, through applying them, develop habits of effective listening?

My answer is that the rules are essentially the same as the rules for effective reading. That should not be surprising. The two processes are alike in what they require the mind to do.

In both, the mind of the receiver—the reader or listener—must somehow penetrate through the words used to the thought that lies behind them. The impediments that language places in the way of understanding must be overcome. The vocabulary of the speaker or writer is seldom if ever identical with the vocabulary of the listener or reader. The latter must always make the effort to get at a meaning that can be expressed in different sets of words. The listener must come to terms with the speaker, just as the reader must come to terms with the writer. This, in effect, means discovering what the idea is regardless of how it is expressed in words.

In listening as in reading, it is necessary to note the statements that convey the main points the speaker or writer is trying to make. Not everything said or written is of equal importance. In most discourses, whether spoken or written, the number of truly important propositions being advanced is relatively small. The listener, like the reader, must detect these and highlight them in his mind, separating them from all the contextual remarks that are interstitial, transitional, or merely elaborative and amplifying.

Like a written document, however long or short, the speech being listened to is a whole that has parts. If it is worth listening to, its structure (the way the parts are organized to form the whole) and its sequence (the way one part leads to or connects with another) will be perspicuous and coherent. Therefore, the listener, like the reader, must make the effort to observe the relation and sequence of the parts as constituting the whole.

Like the writer, the speaker proceeds with some overarching and regulative purpose or intention that controls the substance and style of what is being presented. The sooner the listener, like the reader, perceives the focus of this controlling purpose or intention, the better he or she is able to discriminate between what is of major and what is of minor significance in the discourse that is to be understood.

Understanding what the speaker is trying to say, perceiving how he or she is managing to say it, and noting the reasons given or the arguments advanced for the conclusions that the speaker seeks to have adopted are indispensable to effective listening, just as they are indispensable to effective reading. But they are never enough. With regard to anything that one understands, either by reading or listening, it is always necessary to make up one's own mind about where one stands—either agreeing or disagreeing.

One may be unable to do either because one recognizes that what has been said has not been sufficiently understood to warrant agreement or disagreement. Another reason for withholding agreement or disagreement is that one wishes further elucidations or arguments that have not yet been forthcoming. In either case, the critical listener, like the critical reader, should suspend judgment for the time being, and pursue the matter further at another time.

· 4 ·

In *How to Read a Book*, I set forth the rules for the adequate reading of a book that, because of its substance and style, deserves careful reading. First, there were rules for analyzing the book's structure as a whole and the orderly arrangement of its parts. One should be able to say what the whole book is about and how each of its parts successively contributes to the significance of the whole.

Second, there were rules for interpreting the contents of the book: by discerning the principal terms in the author's conceptual vocabulary, by identifying the author's main propositions or contentions, by recognizing the arguments the author employed in supporting or defending these propositions, and by noting the problems the author through the book solved, as well as the problems the book left unsolved, whether the author knows it or not.

Third, there were rules for criticizing the book by indi-

cating matters about which the author appeared to be uninformed or misinformed, by noting what appeared to be
the author's errors in reasoning from the premises or assumptions that seemed valid, and by observing the respects in which the author's analysis or argument appeared
to be incomplete.

As stated, these rules are obviously intended for reading
an important book—even better, a great book—to which
one is willing to devote a great deal of time and effort because of the profit to be gained.

No speech, however important or extensive, has the
magnitude or complexity of an important or great book.
The rules of reading must, therefore, be simplified and
accommodated to the limitations of oral, as contrasted
with written, discourse.

In addition, one can devote an unlimited amount of time
to the reading and rereading of a book in order to improve
one's understanding of it and to determine one's critical
response to it.

Unlike reading, listening is subject to the limitations of
time. We can only listen once to what is being said to us
and the pace of our listening is determined by the pace set
by the speaker. We cannot stop the speaker and ask him to
repeat something that was said earlier, as we can stop
going forward to the next page to review pages read earlier. We cannot hold up our hand to signal the speaker to
pause while we ponder something he has just said, as we
can put the book down for as long as we wish to ponder
what we have just read.

Other things make active listening much less frequent
than active reading. You do not have to exert any muscu-
lar effort in order to listen, as you do to hold a book in
your hand. This at least gives some semblance of activity

on the part of a reader. You do not have to keep your eyes open to listen, but this you must do to give at least the appearance of reading. You can be completely passive with your eyes closed and with your mind turned off and still pretend that you are listening.

All these differences between listening and reading not only explain why effective listening is much more difficult than effective reading; they also call for a much simpler set of rules to guide us in the effort to use our minds actively in listening well.

The essence of being a good reader is to be a demanding reader. A demanding reader is one who stays awake while reading, and does so by asking questions as he reads. Passivity in reading, which really renders the process null and void, consists in using one's eyes to see the words, but not using one's mind to understand what they mean.

The good listener, like the good reader, is a demanding listener, one who keeps awake while listening by having in mind the questions to be asked about the speech being listened to.

I have formulated elsewhere the four main questions that a demanding reader must ask of anything that is worth the effort to read well, for profit or pleasure, not just to kill time or put oneself to sleep. I will now try to adapt them to listening to a speech.

Listening to a speech, or any other form of spoken utterance, is analogous, in the length of time required, to reading an article or an essay rather than a whole book. Like an article or essay, the speech will be shorter and will be a simpler whole, a less complex organization of parts. Therefore, the questions to be used in listening to a speech can be simpler than the ones recommended for reading a book. Here they are:

i. *What is the whole speech about?* What, in essence, is the speaker trying to say and how does he go about saying it? ii. *What are the main or pivotal ideas, conclusions, and arguments?* What are the special terms used to express these ideas and to state the speaker's conclusions and arguments? iii. *Are the speaker's conclusions sound or mistaken?* Are they well-supported by his arguments, or is that support inadequate in some respect? Was the speaker's thinking carried far enough or were matters that were relevant to his controlling purpose not touched on? iv. *What of it?* What consequences follow from the conclusions the speaker wishes to have adopted? What are their importance or significance for me?

It is possible to have all these questions in mind while listening, but most of us would find it impossible to try to answer them at the same time that we are listening to an ongoing speech. Yet answering them later when reflecting upon what one has listened to is an indispensable adjunct to listening. If these questions cannot be answered as the speech goes on, they must be answered retrospectively when one reflects on what one has listened to.

The active reading of a long book or even a short essay calls for more than the persistent use of one's mind with a maximum effort of attention. It can seldom be done without using pen or pencil, either marking the book itself, writing in the margins or on the end papers, or jotting notes down on a pad that lies beside the book on one's desk.

Since listening to a speech or any other form of oral discourse is intrinsically more difficult than reading a book or an essay, it is even more necessary to put pen or pencil to paper in the process. Skillful listening involves skillful note-taking, both while the speech is going on and after it is over, when one reviews one's notes and reflects on them. Then one should make a new series of notes that is a better record of what one has listened to and how it has affected one's mind.

In *How to Read a Book*, I acknowledged the fact that, though few of us read well enough for the most part, each of us may do a good job of reading in some particular connection, when the stakes are high enough to compel the requisite exertion. To illustrate what I had in mind, I wrote as follows:

The student who is generally superficial may, for a special reason, read some one thing well. Scholars, who are as superficial as the rest of us in most of their reading, often do a careful job when the text is in their own narrow field, especially if their reputations hang on what they say. On cases relevant to his practice, a lawyer is likely to read analytically. A physician may similarly read clinical reports which describe symptoms he is currently concerned with. But both these learned men may make no similar effort in other fields or at other times. Even business assumes the air of a learned profession when its devotees are called upon to examine financial statements or contracts. . . .

If we consider men and women generally, and apart from their professions or occupations, there is only one situation I can think of in which they almost pull themselves up by their bootstraps, making an effort to read better than they usually do. When they are in love and are reading a love letter, they read for all they are worth. They read every word three ways; they read between the lines and in the margins; they read the whole in terms of the parts, and each part in terms of the whole; they grow sensitive to context and ambiguity, to insinuation and implication; they perceive the color of words, the odor of phrases, and the weight of sentences. They may even take the punctuation into account. Then, if never before or after, they read.

What is true of reading is equally true of listening. It is easy to think of occasions when everyone will make the effort required for rapt listening, comparable to the extraordinarily perceptive reading all of us give to a love letter. One illustration should suffice. Others can be readily imagined.

You are a passenger in an airplane travelling over water. The pilot comes on the intercom and says: "This is your captain speaking from the cockpit. We are compelled to make an emergency landing twelve minutes from now. I will describe the procedure and prepare you for it. Please listen carefully. When I am finished, the cabin attendants will walk down the aisle. There will be plenty of time left for you to ask them questions. Do not panic. If you understand and follow instructions, there need be no injuries or loss of life."

Would you not listen with rapt attention and try to understand perfectly; or, failing that, would you not try to ask clear questions and listen to the answers given?

CHAPTER VIII

Writing While and
After Listening

· I ·

Of all the books I have written, *How to Read a Book* has
been most often reprinted since its publication in 1940,
has reached the widest audience, and has elicited what has
been for me the most gratifying expressions of apprecia-
tion from readers whose lives it has affected. It has made
reading for them both more profitable and more pleasurable, and, opening the pages of the great books for them, it
has given them a lifelong pursuit.

Of all the articles I have written, none has been reprinted more frequently in anthologies or textbooks for
students than an essay I wrote in 1941 for *The Saturday
Review*, entitled "How to Mark a Book." *How to Read a
Book* had insisted upon the necessity of actively using one's
mind while reading, always by reading with a questioning
mind. That can be done without pen, pencil, or pad. But
the best way to make sure that you are incessantly active
while reading is by making notes, page by page, as you
read—not in bed or in an armchair, but at a table or desk.

Making notes while reading is highly useful, certainly to
be recommended to anyone who may lapse back into pas-

sive reading, but it is not absolutely necessary. It may not be necessary to make notes while listening if the speech to which you are listening is sufficiently brief. However, if it promises to be fairly long and complex, you would be well advised to bring pencil and paper to the task of listening to it. Unless you can trust your memory more than most of us can, I would recommend making notes, but only if the speech has enough substance and significance for you to make the effort.

Writing while listening is productive and desirable. Talking while listening is counterproductive.

The notes you take while listening record what you have done with your mind to take in what you have heard. That record enables you to go on to the second step, which I regard as equally important to the activity of listening. What you have noted during the course of listening, together with what your memory retains of what was said, provides you with food for thought.

The thinking you then do should lead you to make a second set of notes, much more orderly, much more comprehensive, and much more critical. These concluding notes constitute the completion of the task of active listening. You have used your mind as well as possible in response to what, in the speech you heard, you thought was worthy of attention and comment.

The chief difference between the two sets of notes is that the first must be made at a pace dictated by the speaker while the second can be timed at your own discretion. In addition, the order of what you jot down while listening is determined by the order of what is being said, while you are entirely free to order your second set of notes in whatever way seems best to serve the purpose of getting at the gist of what you heard and expressing your own reaction to it.

There are those who, trying to save themselves time, try to do, while listening, what they should reserve for subsequent reflection. They attempt to jot down their own reactions to what is being said at the same time that they are trying to record what they think the speaker is saying. This not only reduces the accuracy of the record, it also prevents them from hearing much of what has been said. So preoccupied are they with their own thoughts that they pay too little attention to the thoughts expressed by the speaker.

Even if you do not go on to complete the task of listening by making the second set of notes after due reflection at a later time, do not make the mistake of trying to combine your record of what you are hearing with your own reactions to it. Listeners who are more concerned to express themselves than to pay close attention to what someone else is trying to express are very poor listeners—they really wish they were making the speech rather than listening to it.

In earlier chapters I have divided uninterrupted speeches, long or short, into those that aim to affect the conduct of their listeners by persuading them to do something or to feel differently, and those that aim to affect the minds of their listeners by adding to their knowledge, altering their understanding, or getting them to think differently.

I have used the term "sales talk" or persuasive speech for the one, and "lecture" or instructive speech for the other, but the reader should remember that I have tried to use both terms in the broadest possible manner, covering political oratory and business negotiations as well as all forms of marketing under the one, and including under the other all forms of teaching.

Since the way in which we should react to speech that aims at persuading us to act or feel in a certain manner differs markedly from the way in which we should react to speech that aims to change our minds and affect our thinking, it is necessary to deal separately with note-making while listening to persuasive speech and note-making while listening to instructive speech. I will begin with the latter.

· 2 ·

The running notes you make while listening to instructive speech should include at least four different observations on your part.

1. If the speech you are listening to is itself well organized and prepared in a manner that facilitates listening, the speaker will in his opening remarks tell you the ground he proposes to cover. He will indicate in summary fashion the gist of the message he is trying to convey. He may even, if he is a very orderly speaker, tell you at the very beginning how he is going to cover the ground he has laid out for himself and how he is going to proceed, point by point, to develop his central theme, leading up to the conclusion or conclusions he wishes you to share with him.

If that is the case, note-making must begin at the very beginning. Many listeners wait too long before they begin to jot down notes. They are laggardly or dilatory about using their minds for active listening. They are slow in adjusting themselves to the speaker and, as a result, often miss noting what is of prime importance to record.

Not all speakers, of course, are as orderly as they should be, nor do all make the effort to prepare their listeners for the task of listening well by telling them at the very beginning what they should pay particular attention to. Their failures in this respect will be manifested by the rambling and desultory character of their opening remarks.

This should put you on notice that your task of note-making is going to be more difficult. You are going to have to be alert in waiting for the time when the speaker finally gets around to revealing what is on his mind as the main substance of address. You cannot prevent the speaker from wandering, but do not let your own mind wander. Keep your ears cocked for statements by the speaker that, at one moment or another, focus your attention on the central substance of the speech. Take note of them.

2. Once again, if the speaker you are listening to is genuinely concerned to have you understand what is being said he will realize that his conceptual vocabulary—the basic terms of reference he will be using—may be peculiarly his own, and he will make a special effort to call attention to these terms.

When each term is first introduced, the speaker will say, "I am using this word or that in the following manner" or "Please note that when I use the word '———' I am referring to '———.'" By all means, do note what you have been asked to observe. Not to pay attention to the speaker's special use of certain words or phrases is to fail to come to terms with him. That failure on your part is a serious if not fatal obstacle to your understanding what is being said.

Less careful or considerate speakers may use their own private vocabulary without making any effort to call your attention to the crucial terms to which they have attached a special meaning. Then your task as a listener is more difficult, but also more important to discharge. You must make the effort to spot the words or phrases that the speaker is using in a sense that seems strange or unfamiliar to you, or at least that differs from the sense in which you yourself use the same words or phrases. Take note of as many of these as you can.

3. In the course of arguing for the conclusion or conclusions that the speaker wishes you to adopt, a logically sensitive speaker, of which unfortunately there are too few, will lay before you the underlying premises on which his reasoning rests.

Some of these, if not all, will consist of statements that the speaker cannot establish as true beyond a reasonable doubt or with a high degree of probability, certainly not beyond the shadow of a doubt. The time available does not permit the full elucidation of all or most of his underlying premises.

The logically sensitive speaker will ask you to follow his reasoning by accepting his assumptions for the time being—accepting them to discern their consequences, to see how they lead to the conclusions he wishes to arrive at. It is important for you to take note of these assumptions, whether or not the speaker is honest enough to admit that, for the purposes of the occasion, that is all they are, not axioms or self-evident truths, or even adequately supported principles.

Many speakers fail to make their initial premises clear. They fail to call attention to the relatively small number of assertions on which their whole argument rests. They may indicate them obliquely or acknowledge them tacitly.

Your task is to be on the alert to detect the initial premises, the principles, the assumptions that provide the ultimate grounds for what is being said. The task is more difficult to perform if these are concealed rather than revealed, but it is then all the more necessary to discharge.

4. If the speech you are listening to moves in one or another fashion from starting points to conclusions, that motion will consist in some marshalling of reasons, some adduction of evidence, some formulation of arguments, more or less explicitly presented. The more explicitly they are presented, the easier your task of noting the reasons, the evidence, the arguments. But easy or difficult, you must make the effort to jot down in some shorthand fashion a record of how the speaker tried to carry you from his starting points to his conclusions.

Whether or not the speaker has given you advance notice of the conclusions he wishes to leave you with, and whether or not he has been as explicit as he should be in presenting the grounds for reaching these conclusions, you cannot complete your note-making while listening to a speech without making some record of what the conclusions are.

If you have done all of the four foregoing things while the speech is going on, your running notes, more or less orderly and more or less abbreviated, will be a sufficient record of what you have heard to enable you to take the next step, in which you review what you have heard, reflect upon it, and express your own reactions to it.

That need not be done at once. There is seldom the time or the circumstances for doing it then. But if you are going to do it at all, it should not be postponed too long. It can be done better when your memory of what you have heard is fresh, rich, and vivid rather than stale, fragmentary, and dim.

· 3 ·

In making the second set of notes, the following things should be done.

1. First of all, regardless of how orderly or disorderly the speaker has been, you should try to put down on paper as orderly a summary of the speech as you can manage. You can extract the material for his summary from your running notes, embellished by what your memory has retained. Whereas your running notes may have had the brevity of shorthand, your retrospective summary should be spelled out in as much detail as you can achieve.

Ideally, this retrospective summary should amount to a précis of the speaker's own notes, if he had an orderly set of notes before him as the guidelines of his speech. It may even be, in short form, a written record of what was said. It should at least be an accurate and unbiased representation of what was said, even though it may not be a comprehensive account of it.

2. With this summary laid before you (including the speaker's initial premises or assumptions, the words he used in some special sense that were his crucial terms, the conclusions at which he aimed, and the ways in which he tried to support those conclusions) you are in a position to react to what you have heard. Expressing your own reactions is as much a part of actively listening to a speech as it is a part of actively reading a book.

If you understood the speech perfectly and if you agree with its conclusions completely, your only reaction will be to say "Amen." That may happen in a rare case, but it seldom happens in the normal course of events.

a. When this does not happen, your first task is to express in words the things you failed to understand. Why did the speaker say this or that? Why did he think that the reasons or evidence he advanced were adequate to support his conclusions. Why did he fail to comment on objections that might be raised to what he said? What did he mean by this or that word which he used in a special sense without explicitly calling attention to the sense in which he used it?

b. Next, with regard to points or matters concerning which you think you have sufficient understanding of what was said either to agree or disagree with the speaker, you should make some statement of what you agreed with and what you disagreed with. If you wish to be particularly scrupulous about your disagreements, you should indicate your reasons for taking that position. Even with respect to your agreement, it may serve some purpose to note whether it rests on the reasons given by the speaker or is grounded also on additional reasons of your own.

c. Agreement or disagreement may not always follow an understanding of what you have heard. You may find that the speaker's support for his conclusions is inadequate in some respect and you may not be able yourself to provide the support needed either to affirm or to deny the conclusions in question. Under these circumstances, you should record yourself as suspending judgment. That leaves more work to be done, by yourself or someone else, before you can make up your mind about the matters in question.

d. Whether you agree, disagree, or suspend judgment, there is one more thing to do in response to the speech you have listened to. Supposing the speaker is correct in his conclusions and supposing that they can be adequately supported, it still remains to ask "What of it?" That question can also be asked on the opposite supposition; namely, that the speaker's conclusions are incorrect and that sufficient support can be found for a contrary set of conclusions. This final question, asked in either case, involves you in thinking about the significance for you of the speech as a whole.

If these recommendations for note-making while listening to a speech and note-making when you have time later to reflect upon what you have heard seem excessively elaborate and painstaking, they should be followed only to the extent that the character and substance of the speech is rich and important enough to deserve all the effort called for.

There are, of course, many uninterrupted speeches that are so trivial in content, so disorderly in presentation, and so incoherent in general that they do not deserve careful listening, much less the kind of active listening that involves making notes.

The precept of prudence in following the recommendations suggested is simply to make whatever adaptation or use of them the substance, style, and importance of the speech deserves, making the maximum effort for the best of speeches, less for those that are less worthy, and none at all for those that were not worth listening to in the first place.

If the speech, however important and excellent, is relatively brief, then close and active listening to it calls for fewer and briefer notes than those indicated above. It may even be that what the memory can retain of a relatively short speech suffices for making retrospective and reflective notes about it after it is over, without having to make running notes while it is going on.

· 4 ·

When you are listening to a sales talk, to political oratory of any kind, to commercial appeals, or to exhortations by business executives, all of whom speak with the purpose of getting you to do something or to feel one way rather than another, it is important for you to have a reasonable degree of sales resistance. Don't be a pushover for persuasion, but at the same time do not erect insuperable barriers to being moved by it.

Active listening to uninterrupted speech of this general kind is usually less exacting than listening actively to speech that is essentially instructive rather than persuasive. Nevertheless, it may be useful to make a few brief notes while listening. These should usually take the form of questions to which answers should be forthcoming.

1. What is the speaker trying to sell, or, in other words, what is he trying to get me to do or get me to feel?

2. Why does the speaker think I should be persuaded by this appeal? What reasons are offered or what facts are presented in support of this appeal?

3. What points that I think are relevant has the speaker failed to mention? What has he failed to say that might sway me one way or the other?

4. When the speaker has completed his persuasive effort, what questions of significance to me has he failed to answer, or even consider?

If, on one or more of the foregoing counts, the speaker has failed to satisfy you, so that you are left unable to answer these questions or are left in serious doubt about what the answers are, you should remain unpersuaded. This does not mean that you are unpersuadable about the matter at hand, but only that more must be done to overcome your justified sales resistance and to turn you into a buyer, a complier, or an accomplice of some kind.

In my judgment, it is seldom the case that an attempt to persuade can be carried to a successful conclusion by uninterrupted speech. Such speech must usually be supplemented by what I have called two-way talk—an interchange between speaker and listener, in which one asks questions and the other answers them.

The notes made while listening serve to facilitate this question and answer session, which should begin when the speech is over.

The person engaged in persuasion should be as anxious and ready to engage in two-way talk as the audience being addressed. He can reinforce and drive home crucial points by answering the questions put to him by his listeners. He can assuage doubts and overcome objections by doing this skillfully—and honestly!

In addition, he can make his original appeal more effectively persuasive by asking his listeners questions that may bring to the fore points of resistance they have kept in the background, or by posing, and then at once answering, questions that lurked in the back of his listeners' minds.

In this way, he can deal with and try to overcome half-formulated or even hidden objections.

· 5 ·

What is true of uninterrupted speech that aims at persuasion is equally true of uninterrupted speech that aims at instruction. From the point of view of listeners to the latter kind of speech, the two-way talk of a question and answer session provides an opportunity for getting answers to questions that they have raised in their notes or for posing objections to what the speaker has said to which they would like to hear the speaker's response. As a result, they may cease to suspend judgment, or change their minds from disagreement to agreement, or perhaps the reverse. In any case, the question and answer session will serve to fulfill the efforts they made to listen as actively as possible.

Speakers who seek to instruct also profit from engaging in the two-way talk of a forum or question and answer session after the speech is finished. Without it, they can seldom if ever be sure that what they have tried to say has been well listened to, nor can they make a reasonable estimate of how far they succeeded in affecting the minds of their audience in the way they wished. Only by submitting to the questions the audience poses or the objections it raises can speakers correct misunderstandings that have occurred, repeat what should have been heard but may not have been heard at all, and supplement what they have said by introducing points that they should have made but failed to make in the first place.

In addition, speakers themselves may wish to use the occasion of a forum or a question and answer session to ask the audience questions, specifically for the purpose of finding out whether they have been understood, what difficulties they have failed to consider, what objections may lie hidden in the listeners' minds.

Uninterrupted speech and silent listening, even when they are done as well as possible, seldom serve the ultimate purpose of communication, which is the meeting of minds in such a way that they share a common understanding, whether or not they agree or disagree. Such speech and listening should always, or wherever possible, be followed by two-way talk, the kind of interchange between speakers and listeners that is conversation or discussion.

Only through conversation or discussion can speaking and listening be consummated and rendered as fruitful as they should be. This is the kind of speaking and listening to which we now turn in the next part of this book. There we shall first of all treat the forum or question and answer session that should follow uninterrupted speech and silent listening.

PART FOUR

Two-Way Talk

CHAPTER IX

Question and Answer Sessions: Forums

· I ·

Up to this point, we have been dealing separately with two halves, speaking and listening, that should be fitted together.

Writing and reading are almost always separated from one another. There is seldom any way for readers to test their understanding of a book by direct interrogation of the author. Nor can authors often ascertain how well their books have been read by submitting to questions from their readers. It is a rare book review that serves that purpose, though sometimes letters from readers do.

In contrast to writing and reading, speaking and listening are frequently conjoined in an interchange, a face-to-face transaction in which speaker and listener alternate in asking and answering questions. As I have already pointed out, neither kind of speech—the kind that aims at instruction and the kind that aims at persuasion for some practical purpose—can be as effective as it should be unless it is followed by a question and answer session.

This conclusion is attested to in the political life of the ancient world by the centrality in public affairs of the

Athenian agora and the Roman forum. These open spaces for the gathering of the citizens were not only places where political speeches were made, but also places where the citizens reacted to the speaker, asking questions and responding to answers. The word "forum" has come down to us from antiquity as the name for any gathering at which a speaker submits to interrogation from his audience.

In British political life, even today in the era of television, candidates for Parliament take to the hustings, which means that they go to public places not merely to harangue the electorate, but also to face a barrage of questions that they are called upon to answer. In Parliament itself, there are regular question periods when members of the government who have delivered state papers face questions from the party in opposition.

In the United States, the use of television has reduced the number of occasions for direct confrontations in which candidates face the people and the challenge of their questions or their objections. In the old days, presidential candidates toured the country by train, speaking at one whistle stop after another to track-side gatherings and responding to questions or other challenges. That is no longer the case, and something valuable has been lost, both for the candidates and for the public.

The forum is just as useful an adjunct to speeches that are not oratorical and political in purpose. In London, at Hyde Park Corner on Sunday afternoons, speakers take to soap boxes to deliver speeches on a wide variety of theoretical subjects, ranging from the existence of God and the immortality of the soul to the evils of vivisection and the merits of birth control by contraception or abortion. They always attract a crowd of people, young and old, who come there not merely to listen to the speakers, but to pepper them with questions when they have finished.

There is nothing quite like Hyde Park Corner in the United States, but there has been a long tradition in this country of public lectures that are advertised as including a question and answer period. The Chautauqua lecture series at the end of the last century and the beginning of this one is a case in point. The Ford Hall Forum in Boston and the Cooper Union Forum in New York are two well-known examples of this practise of gathering an audience not only to listen but to ask.

· 2 ·

My own experience as a lecturer began in the twenties at Cooper Union in New York. The question and answer period that followed the lecture was given equal time: it went on for an hour following a lecture that occupied an hour. The audience would have dwindled to almost nothing if that were not the case. They listened to lectures in order to pit themselves against the lecturer by posing the most difficult questions they could contrive or raising objections they thought might stump him.

This made them better listeners, for they soon learned that if the questions they asked or the objections they raised revealed their inattention to what the lecturer had said or their misunderstanding of it, they would be bluntly put down as out of order. Politeness or civility did not restrain the chairman of the proceedings from being a disciplinarian who demanded that listeners prove by the questions they asked that they were coming to bat or were at least in the ball park and not somewhere else.

That well-conducted or well-regulated forum not only improved the listening and tested the mettle of the listeners, it also taught the speakers much that they could not have learned in any other way. I discovered this very early in my experience as a frequent lecturer at the Cooper Union Forum. The discovery has been confirmed over and over again ever since, during the fifty years or more in which I have addressed public audiences under the widest variety of auspices and student audiences in diverse types of educational institutions.

I deeply regret the occasions when limited time or other circumstances have prevented me from answering questions or meeting objections raised by the audience. I have learned nothing just from hearing myself speak, totally deprived of any sense about whether what I have said has been adequately heard and understood. I might just as well have been speaking in an empty hall.

When a forum follows the lecture—and the longer the question and answer session the better—I learn a great deal about what I have said. I learn which of my terms need greater clarification. I learn what assumptions need to be more fully explicated. I learn what points need further elucidation and why it is necessary to change the order in which certain points are made. I learn where one argument needs amplification and another can be improved by stating it more succinctly.

That is not all I learn. I also learn from objections raised and difficulties posed where my own thinking has been mistaken or inadequate. Objections I cannot satisfactorily meet call for serious emendations of the lecture I have given. Questions that I cannot satisfactorily answer call for additions that must be made—points added, clarifications advanced.

All this learning that a forum contributes to my thinking improves the lecture the second time I give it, and so on for the third, fourth, and successive occasions, until the profit I reap from further question and answer sessions becomes relatively negligible. Then I know that I have sufficiently tested my thinking and speaking so that I can be relatively sure that what I have thought and said about the subject has become generally intelligible and generally acceptable, even if it falls short of perfection, as it always will. Later occasions, when some new question or unexpected objection is raised, are a constant reminder of this fact.

I regard the learning provided by the lecture-forum experience, repeated many times, as so valuable that in the last forty years most of the books I have written have been expansions of lectures that have undergone the testing, the learning, and the detailed improvements in both substance and style that have resulted from speaking to listeners who talk back.

How to Read a Book was the first book I wrote that way, and it was much better than the earlier books I had written as if I were talking only to myself in the silence of my study. I had given a lecture on the art of reading to many and diverse audiences a full year or more before I sat down to write it out. The lecture had undergone many revisions, both emendations and expansions. My file of lecture notes and other notes, made as a result of facing audiences, was what produced the book. Its success in reaching a wide audience of readers persuaded me to adopt the same procedure for the writing of subsequent books.

I would almost dare to say that speaking and listening, when properly conjoined in a lecture-forum, is the best way to write a book. Other things may be necessary adjuncts as well, but the author who has not faced audiences, who has not learned from their questions and objections what must be done to improve his thought and what must be said to communicate it effectively, is deprived of input he can acquire in no other way.

If I may pursue my personal reminiscences a bit further, I would like to add that the lecture-forum arrangements at St. John's College in Annapolis and under the auspices of the Aspen Institute for Humanistic Studies have been the most fruitful occasions of learning for me, involving both a student audience and a public audience. I would like to think that they have been equally fruitful occasions of learning for the audiences involved.

At St. John's College, there is one formal lecture a week given to the whole college, with compulsory attendance for the student body. When the lecture is concluded in the auditorium and after a brief break, the members of the student body reassemble in the discussion room. The question and answer session never runs less than a hour and a half and often much longer.

The students learn from me points they have missed and points they have misunderstood, and our diverse conceptual vocabularies gradually get adjusted to one another. I learn from the students points I have failed to consider, arguments I have failed to make clear, and mistakes or inadequacies in my own thinking about the subject.

The lecture-forum is an essential part of the learning experience at St. John's College. It is not an optional, extracurricular activity as it is at most colleges and universities, where attendance is voluntary and often sparse and where the question and answer session is usually brief and participated in by only some of the audience. That is why I find lecturing at St. John's College more profitable to me than lecturing at most other educational institutions. The students there have been trained in the discipline of discussion. They have learned how to listen to a lecture in order to engage in the forum that follows it.

The Aspen experience is similar in that the audience attending lectures given there anticipate auditing or participating in the discussion that follows it. They are listeners who look forward to testing themselves and the speaker by the interchanges that occur during the question and answer period. The intellectual quality of the audience and the diversity of scholarly or professional backgrounds from which they come make the Aspen lecture-forum more profitable than most, both for speakers and listeners.

In the early years of the Aspen Institute, when its schedule of seminars, conferences, lectures, and other activities was less crowded and so allowed more time for forums, the arrangement for those was ideal in my judgment. Instead of having the question and answer period in the auditorium immediately after the lecture, the audience reassembled in another room the next morning. The forum that was then conducted ran for a full two hours and involved, in addition to the lecturer of the evening before, a panel of other persons who had some special competence to deal with the questions or objections that the lecture evoked.

The advantage of this procedure was that it gave the audience time to examine the notes they might have taken during the lecture, to reflect on them or on their memory of what had been said, and even to formulate carefully the questions or objections they wished to present. As a result, the questions were more thoughtful, the objections were better reasoned, snap judgments and irrelevant remarks were eliminated, and the discussion, with the help of the panel that assisted the speaker, was better conducted.

I wish it were always possible to postpone the forum that should follow a lecture until the morning after, but unfortunately I have never again had the pleasurable and profitable experience provided by the lecture-forum arrangements in the early years of the Aspen Institute.

· 3 ·

How should a forum, under any circumstances, be conducted? Let me answer that question first from the point of view of the speaker, and then from the point of view of the listeners.

If given the opportunity, the speaker would do well to control the discussion by a device that I have always used at St. John's College and sometimes at Aspen. He should open the forum by asking the listeners who are going to participate to distinguish between questions that seek for a further or better understanding of what has been said and questions that challenge the speaker. The first type of question should precede all others, for there is no point in trying to answer questions or meet objections that arise from misunderstandings.

This first type of question should take the following form: "Do I understand you to say that . . . ?" The speaker can then respond by stating that the questioner has either understood or has not. In the latter case, the speaker can then make an effort to clarify what was said in order to produce the understanding that was lacking. Only after all such questions have been answered and the speaker is satisfied that he has been sufficiently understood, is it proper and profitable for him to try to answer questions that challenge what he has said or that pose objections to this or that point in his thought about the subject. Questions seeking information about what has been said or testing the listener's understanding of it should always precede challenges and objections.

Sometimes listeners will preface their questions by attributing to the speaker statements that either did not occur in the speech or are serious misrepresentations of what was actually said. "You said such and such," the questioner will begin. I always raise my hand or shake my head to tell the questioner at once that I did not make the statement that he just expressed. There is no point in considering a question about something that I did not say or about a distorted version of what I said. I then repeat what I did say and ask my questioner whether that provokes a question in his mind.

There are two other things that the speaker can do to facilitate or advance the discussion of his speech. One is to improve the questions asked by rephrasing them in a way that accords better with the substance of the speech. "Let me see if I understand the question you are asking," I will say, "and let me do so by restating your question as follows." When I have done that, I seek approval of my restatement, and only when I have gained it, do I go on to answer the question.

It is often the case that the listener has a good question in mind but is inept in phrasing it. Sometimes a question is thrown wildly at the target rather than being carefully directed. Here again a reformulation of the question by the speaker helps to advance the discussion instead of allowing it to wander far afield.

The other thing the speaker can do is to turn about and become a questioner. This is best done toward the end of

the forum when questions from the audience begin to pe-
ter out. If the speaker feels that there are good questions
that have not been asked and that he would like to answer
in order to elucidate what has been said, there is no reason
why he should refrain from posing such questions and answering them.

This last device is particularly useful in making a sales
talk, a political speech, or any other effort at persuasion
for a practical purpose. The persuader should, of course,
try to answer all the questions that indicate resistance to
his appeal. But he would be ill-advised to stop there. Some
of the most important obstacles to the success of his effort
may lie hidden or remain unexpressed in the minds of his
listeners. If he does not ferret them out and answer them,
he may fail to overcome the resistance he is meeting without knowing why.

In addition, the persuader should resort to rhetorical
questions about the matter under consideration, so skillfully phrased that he has reasonable assurance of getting
affirmative answers to them.

In politics, in business negotiations, in selling, delivering a persuasive speech is never enough. It should always
be followed by a question and answer session in which the
persuader can both answer questions raised by his audience and raise questions, especially good rhetorical questions, that elicit the answers he wishes to get from them.

· 4 ·

From the point of view of the listener who plans to participate in a discussion of what he or she has heard,
whether that is a speech that aims to instruct or one that
aims to persuade, the notes taken while listening should

provide the basis of the questions to be asked. In the absence of such notes, what the memory retains will have to suffice.

When instruction is the purpose of the speech, listeners should have two objectives in mind. One is to be sure that they fully understand what they have heard. The other is to challenge the speaker in such a way that they can decide whether to agree or disagree with what has been said about this point or that.

Where persuasion is the purpose of the speech, listeners should use the opportunity to question the speaker in order to draw attention to highly relevant considerations that the speaker purposely failed to deal with, omitted because the persuader feared they might arouse resistance to his efforts. In addition, listeners may wish to make sure that they have heard correctly the reasons offered for doing this or that, and if those reasons seem insufficient, listeners then have an opportunity to raise objections to the appeal and see if they can be answered.

The person who is persuaded in the political arena, in business conferences and negotiations, or in the marketplace is one who feels secure that all relevant considerations have been covered and all pertinent questions have been answered. He may be deluded in thinking so and that may be his own fault as a listener and a questioner.

The person who is left with questions that the persuader fails to answer or objections that he fails to meet, is likely to be one who, for good reasons, remains unpersuaded.

CHAPTER X

The Variety
of Conversations

· I ·

Forums following instructive lectures or persuasive speeches are just one kind of conversation and discussion. It is a very special kind because such question and answer sessions draw their substance from a speech made and listened to and they take direction from the purpose that motivated the speech. There are many other types of direct interchanges between speakers and listeners confronting one another, remarkably diverse in motivation and character, ranging from cocktail party chitchat and dinner table chatter to the most serious of political debates and business conferences and the most exalted university seminars and scholarly symposia.

In order to set forth the rules for making different types of conversation more pleasurable and profitable, it is necessary to classify them, noting the characteristics that distinguish them from one another. We must do so for the same reason that we found it necessary earlier to distinguish the two main types of uninterrupted speech—the persuasive and the instructive—and to consider the differences in the role of the listener with respect to each.

I propose the following fourfold classification of the types of two-way talk—the kinds of conversation. It is convenient for our purposes even if it is probably not exhaustive.

· 2 ·

The first division is between playful and serious conversations. By playful conversation, I mean all forms of talk that have no set purpose, no objective to achieve, no controlling direction. In addition, like play itself, which is that form of human activity in which we engage purely for the pleasure inherent in the activity itself, conversation that is playful in intent rather than seriously motivated is conversation that is enjoyable for its own sake, and not pursued for any ulterior purpose.

Another name for this kind of talk is "social conversation." It is the easy, informal talk that takes place in pleasant companionship with one's friends or associates. It may be informative, but it need not be, nor need it be enlightening though it may also be that. It simply gives pleasure and, by doing so, it brings persons together in friendship or helps to make them better acquainted with one another.

A good social conversation can never be planned in advance. It just happens if the circumstances fortuitously favor its occurring. To set in advance what is to be discussed is to plan something akin to a business meeting. Social conversation should be permitted to wander. There is no goal to reach, nothing to decide.

The remaining three types of conversation, according to this scheme of classification, are all serious rather than playful. They are purposeful and directed. Here the major division is between conversations that are essentially and intimately personal and those that are impersonal.

What I have in mind when I use the phrase "personal conversation" is often called a "heart-to-heart talk." All of us can recall one or another occasion in our lives when we have said to someone near and dear to us, "Let's have a heart-to-heart talk about that."

The phrase "heart-to-heart talk" can be misleading if it is misinterpreted to mean that we engage in such talk using our hearts rather than our minds. All talk, playful or serious, personal or impersonal, involves the exercise of the mind. But the so-called heart-to-heart talk is one in which we use our minds to talk to one another about things that affect our hearts—our emotions and feelings, our affections and disaffections.

Suck talk is concerned with emotional problems of deep concern to the persons involved. It is deeply serious, probably more serious than any other kind of talk, for it aims to remove emotional misunderstandings or to alleviate, if not eliminate, emotional tensions.

The two remaining types of talk, both serious, are impersonal rather than personal. One can be called theoretical because it aims to effect a change of mind. It is instructive if the persons involved acquire knowledge they did not have. It is enlightening if they come to understand what they did not understand before, or come to a better understanding of the matters considered.

The talk is practical if it aims at the adoption of a course of action, the making of a decision that affects action, or the alteration of emotional attitudes and impulses that may have consequences for subsequent action. When it deals with emotions and impulses for the practical purpose of selling merchandise, of winning political support, of getting a business plan or policy adopted, the talk is still impersonal rather than personal.

The persuader of others with some practical purpose in view usually plays upon the emotions of those whom he is trying to persuade. His own emotions may not be involved *except for the purpose at hand*. But in the personal or heart-to-heart talk, the emotions of all the parties involved come into play in direct confrontation. It is the kind of talk that occurs between husband and wife, parents and children, members of a family, lovers and friends—never between persons who do not have intimate relationships with one another that bind them together emotionally.

The seller and buyer are not thus related, nor are the business executive and his associates, nor those who talk with one another to achieve some political goal. They are usually strangers or mere acquaintances. Even if they happen to be friends, the ties of friendship and love do not enter into the picture. If, in rare instances, the persons involved in such talk have an emotional intimacy that affects their dealing with one another, this unduly complicates matters for them by introducing constraints and impediments which skew this type of conversation from its normal course.

The personal or heart-to-heart talk usually involves two persons or at most only a few. It usually takes place under circumstances that are private rather than public. It is never the kind of talk that the persons involved would wish to have recorded in the minutes of the meeting, nor is it conducted by having a prepared agenda for the occasion. It may happen spontaneously without preparation, or it may be planned by one person and proposed to the other with a time and place appointed or set for its occurrence. However it happens, it is always a signally significant event in their lives, affecting them and no one else.

Impersonal talk, either instructive or persuasive, may involve two persons, a few, or a larger group. If the persons involved have been associated with one another for some time, that association will affect the ease with which they can communicate with one another. They will have some acquaintance with one another's vocabularies, one another's intellectual commitments, one another's assumptions or prejudices. If they come together for the first time and converse as strangers, they face obstacles to effective communication that must be surmounted and are often difficult to overcome.

In personal or heart-to-heart talks, the persons involved face each other as equals. Even when the inequality of age or maturity is present, as in heart-to-heart talks between parents and children, friendship or love tends to level the participants and is usually facilitated by ignoring such inequality as exists.

Not so with any form of impersonal talk. Here it makes a great difference whether or not the persons engaged confront each other as equals. The usual business conference is a case in point. So, too, is the seminar in which a teacher conducts a discussion with students, or in which the moderator or chairman of a discussion plays a role that is different from that played by the other participants.

The first kind of talk, the playful kind that I have called "social conversation," can take place most effectively in relatively small groups. The best is often just between two persons, but the group can be slightly larger. It is a matter of common observation that when the group exceeds five or six persons, it usually breaks up into two quite separate conversations.

Let me summarize my fourfold classification of the kinds of talk in the following diagram.

PLAYFUL VS. SERIOUS CONVERSATIONS

PERSONAL VS. IMPERSONAL CONVERSATIONS

THEORETICAL VS. PRACTICAL CONVERSATIONS

This gives us four main types, as follows: (1) social conversation; (2) the personal, heart-to-heart talk; (3) the impersonal, theoretical talk that is instructive or enlightening; and (4) the impersonal, practical talk that is persuasive with respect to action.

· 3 ·

Impersonal conversations may be formal or informal, or prepared for or arranged on the one hand or of spontaneous origin on the other hand. The subject to be discussed may be some reading matter that has been assigned, some idea, plan, or policy proposed for consideration, or some problem to be solved, some issue to be resolved, some disagreement or difference of opinion to be overcome.

If the disagreement or difference of opinion is about a matter of fact, it is worth discussing only if the discussion takes the form of considering what consequences flow from one set of facts rather than another, the opposing sets of facts being treated hypothetically for the sake of discussion. Discussion can advance an understanding of the practical or theoretical significance of *supposing* one set of facts to obtain rather than another; but it cannot ever *decide* which is the actual state of affairs with regard to matters of fact. Inquiry, investigation, or research, even if it amounts to no more than going to a reference book to look up the facts in question, is the only way to settle the matter.

For impersonal conversations that have a theoretical purpose, ideas and issues constitute the ideal subject-matter. For those that have a practical purpose, well-formulated plans, policies, and problems provide the richest material.

Practical two-way talk may also be motivated by one person trying to get another or others to do something—to act in a certain way, to move in a certain direction, to become an accomplice in a certain undertaking, to cooperate in this or that enterprise, even to activate sympathy for a certain emotional attitude or disposition.

It also makes a difference whether just two persons are engaged in talk with one another, or the talk involves more than two, and, if more than two, whether one person acts somehow as moderator of the discussion or it proceeds without any control or direction exerted by some member of the group.

Time and place are conditioning circumstances that affect the character of conversations or discussions. These may have to be conducted within time limits or without any such limitations, even to the extent of being carried forward on successive occasions, one after another. The place may be appropriate or inappropriate according to whether it provides an environment that facilitates discussion or one that allows all sorts of distractions or interferences to impede it.

Finally, it must be pointed out that the most important difference between impersonal talks that have a theoretical purpose and those that have a practical purpose lies in the fact that the first can be interminable and inconclusive, whereas the second must be terminated by some conclusion or decision. This is like the difference between a comic and a tragic play. A comedy actually comes to an end with the last act, but in principle it could go on forever. What happens in the last act of a tragedy leaves nothing further to happen.

Since some action to be taken is the goal of practical discussions, they must reach a decisive conclusion and they must usually reach it in a limited time. But when ideas are being discussed or theoretical issues are being disputed, the quest for mutual understanding and agreement can go on interminably, as can the effort to resolve disagreements or reconcile merely apparent differences of opinion.

Such discussions can end at a given time inconclusively, as do many of Plato's dialogues, which are intellectual comedies. The subject may be taken up another time, and still another, and perhaps some conclusions may be reached, but it is never necessary that it be reached at any given time. No practical necessity requires that.

The one exception is, of course, the formal debate, which is conducted within strict time limits and concludes with a vote in favor of one side or the other. Formal debates may be useful in the practical sphere, where a decisive conclusion is sought. They may be useful also in the theoretical sphere, as were the disputations conducted at mediaeval universities.

· 4 ·

In the following chapters I am going to try to formulate rules and suggest factors or conditions that can improve all forms of conversation, making all more pleasurable and the serious ones more profitable.

In Chapter 11, I will deal with the rules and recommendations that can have a salutary effect on conversation in general, as well as on different types of conversation, beginning first with social conversation and dealing then with impersonal discussions, both theoretical and practical.

I will not suggest rules or recommendations for conducting personal conversations—heart-to-heart talks. Precisely because they are personal, and so dependent on the individual temperaments of the persons involved and the emotional circumstances of the moment, they are idiosyncratic. The most that can be said is that, if the persons engaged in such conversations for the sake of emotional clarification are bound by ties of love and friendship, they should be able to conduct them with utter frankness and with nothing withheld because they can do so without fear of misunderstanding or disaffection. Friendship and love rule deception out, both self-deception and deception of the other. They smooth the way to mutual sympathy and insight not only into what deeply concerns the other, but also into one's own deep concern.

In Chapter 12, I will consider what is involved in achieving the ultimate goal of all impersonal talks—the mutual understanding and agreement that constitute a genuine meeting of minds.

I have reserved for separate treatment in Chapter 13 a consideration of the educational significance of discussion, of teaching by asking or questioning instead of by telling, at the level of basic schooling as well as in more advanced institutions.

This kind of teaching is rarely if ever done in the first twelve years of schooling. It should play an essential part there for all twelve years. It is seldom done as well as it can be done in our colleges, or in seminars for adults who wish to continue learning long after they have completed their schooling.

Socratic teaching—teaching by questioning and through discussion—is the most difficult kind of teaching, as well as the most rewarding for everyone involved. Useful rules can be proposed and recommendations made for maximizing the beneficial effects of such teaching. I will try to formulate them in the chapter devoted to the seminar.

CHAPTER XI

How to Make Conversation Profitable and Pleasurable

· I ·

There are certain rules of sufficient generality to be applicable to serious conversations of every sort. There are also certain factors that are operative in such conversations, factors that must be taken into account, for they represent difficulties or obstacles to be overcome. Let us consider these first of all. I will come later to rules for improving social conversations.

Language is the instrument that we use, and must use for the most part, in communicating with one another. If language were a perfect or translucent medium through which one person could see into the mind of another, it would facilitate human conversation to the point where it closely resembled the perfect telepathy of angels. Unfortunately, language is the very opposite. It is a very imperfect medium of communication—cloudy, obscure, full of ambiguities and pitfalls of misunderstanding.

It is almost impossible for any of us to use important words that will be understood by those with whom we talk, particularly words of crucial significance for us, in exactly the same sense in which we use them. Even when we make a special effort to call attention to the meaning we attach to an important word, our cautionary remark often goes unheard, and the response our questions or statements elicit from the person with whom we are conversing reveals that he or she either has not heard or has not paid attention.

Of course, persons engaged in conversation can be expected to use words in a number of different senses. Everyone wants to use words his or her own way. This cannot be changed, but something can be done about it. We can take note of the different senses in which the same word is used and even label them. That takes more care and patience than most people are willing to exert for the sake of making their conversations more communicative, but unless it is done, misunderstandings and even apparently irreconcilable conflicts are bound to result.

Two things would facilitate our overcoming the obstacles that the imperfect medium of language puts in our way. One is a common, general schooling that included intensive training in the liberal arts of grammar, rhetoric, and logic. The other is a common tradition of learning, a background of common reading, an understanding of a relatively small number of basic ideas. Both of these things our ancestors enjoyed, especially in the eighteenth century and down to the end of the nineteenth century. We are for the most part deprived of both by the deterioration of our educational system and by the rampant specialization that abounds in the twentieth century.

Our ancestors were better trained in the liberal arts— the arts of communication as well as the skills of learning. Those who had a proper schooling and, through it, were able to become generally educated persons shared a common literary heritage that endowed them with a common vocabulary, not only of words but also of ideas. This made them members of the same intellectual community, sharing a common background of ideas, references, and allusions. That made communication between them easier and better.

The educated person in the twentieth century is no longer a generalist! He is a specialist, an expert in this field or that. The language of a specialist includes many terms that are the peculiar jargon of his trade, not shared by specialists in other fields. In the twentieth century, well-educated persons, or perhaps I should say those who have had all the schooling available up through college and university, may come out of all that schooling with very little common background in books that all of them have read. This produces what Ortega y Gasset has called "the barbarism of specialization"—the antithesis of the culture of civilization.

A second factor to be controlled for the sake of serious conversations that are impersonal is the heat of emotion. This is not the case in heart-to-heart talks, where emotions are the very substance of discussion. Emotions also have a place in talk that aims to be persuasive in some practical way, but when that is well done, they are manipulated and controlled for the purpose at hand.

However, emotions are entirely out of place in impersonal conversations that have as their goal the achievement of better understanding and the attainment of agreement about the resolution of purely intellectual issues.

The intrusion of emotions into such conversations spoils them, turns them into emotional conflicts when they should be purely intellectual confrontations. As a result, they become battles between conflicting prejudices instead of interchanges that strive for a meeting of minds about ideas or about genuinely disputable opinions, where the dispute can be settled by the adduction of evidence and the marshalling of reasons.

Self-knowledge is still another factor that, when present, facilitates intelligent conversation and, when absent, impedes and frustrates it. Understanding one's self is a necessary condition for understanding anyone else. One should be at least able to talk clearly to oneself. Such clarity in soliloquy is indispensable to clarity in dialogue. Those who lack the insight that is required for intelligent conversation with themselves can scarcely be expected to have the insight needed for intelligent conversation with others.

Last but not least is the amount of effort that must be expended to make any serious conversation worthwhile, both with respect to the profit that can be derived from it and also with respect to the pleasure that can be experienced from conducting it well. Saying what you mean is one of the hardest things in the world to do. Listening to what others say in order to discern what they mean is equally hard. Both call for expenditures of intellectual energy that many persons are loath to make. Such persons are lazy or indolent talkers and their intellectual sloth is one of the cardinal sins that, unrepented and uncorrected, bars the way to achieving the goods that energetically conducted conversation can bestow.

Most of us make the effort required only when the need is pressing and great—either for love or money. If we felt an equally great and pressing need for the meeting of minds, we might make the effort required for thoughtful conversation that aims at mutual understanding and some measure of agreement, or at least of understood disagreement.

Let us turn now to some general rules applicable to all types of serious conversation. Some of these also apply to playful, social conversation, which I will deal with presently.

1. Pick the right place and occasion for a conversation, one that provides sufficient time for carrying it on and one that is free from the annoyance of distractions that interrupt or divert it.

There are times for small talk and times, so to speak, for big talk. A cocktail or dinner party is seldom a place for serious conversation. Whenever conversation must be larded in between other activities, such as going to the theater or going to bed, it might just as well be playful or social. You must always have plenty of time. Good talk is usually slow in getting started and long in winding up. A gathering in which many of those present are strangers is usually a small-talk group. An evening of relaxation, when most of those present are tired, is no occasion to solve the problems of the world. But when friends or acquaintances are present and they share an impulse to discuss problems that have a common interest for them, then serious and even protracted discussion can take place.

Not all occasions are appropriate for good conversation. When you walk into the office of a man with whom you hope to spend an hour or so in serious conversation, and you find him preoccupied with something that happened that day, either in the concerns of his business or of his family, that is hardly an occasion when you can expect to have his full attention.

There is one way to make a dinner party involving more than six persons, some of whom are relative strangers to one another, an occasion for good conversation. I am indebted to my friend Douglass Cater for introducing me to this device.

When the small talk has dwindled and died away, Douglass turns the occasion into one at which big talk may occur, by taking the floor and posing a question to which he solicits answers from everyone, proceeding in round-robin fashion. After everyone has expressed himself or herself on the subject chosen, Douglass continues to chair the meeting by moderating the spirited interchanges that ensue from the differences of opinion expressed. This always turns out to be an enjoyable and profitable experience for everyone concerned.

The other device for turning a dinner party into an occasion for instructive conversation is for the host to ask one of the guests to deliver a short speech on some subject that the host knows will provide substance for a good discussion. The speaker may then be called upon to answer questions from the others present, or the others may make comments on the speech that challenge what has been said.

2. Know in advance what kind of conversation you are trying to have. The first rule for reading a book well is to know what kind of book it is that you are trying to read. Reading a novel is a different exercise from reading a history, and both are different from reading a philosophical work or a scientific treatise.

As we have seen, serious conversations also differ from one another in the substance of what is to be discussed and in the purpose or aim of the discussion. Be aware of the character of the conversation in which you are going to be engaged, whether it is to be theoretical or practical and what its objective is in either case.

3. For whatever kind of serious conversation it is to be, select the right people with whom to have it. Don't try to discuss everything with everybody. Even some of your best friends may lack competence on certain subjects, or interest in them. Sometimes it is not competence or interest that is lacking, but affinity of temperament and some degree of personal affection. If you happen to know that Green and Robinson dislike each other, don't engage them in a conversation that will elicit only their emotional antagonisms.

All of us have had the experience of broaching a theme that is inappropriate for discussion by the persons assembled. When you make that mistake, the conversation falls dead as a doornail, or it wanders away from the theme proposed to gossip or small talk about the weather, the headlines, or sporting events.

Most important of all, never engage in the discussion of a problem with someone you know in advance has a closed mind on that subject. When you know that someone is unpersuadable, don't try to persuade him. When you know that someone is incorrigibly convinced about the truth of this or that position, don't try to change his mind by discussing the question or issue on which he has resolutely and irremediably committed himself to one answer or taken one side. He will remain deaf to all arguments for another answer to the question or another side of the issue.

A judicious selection of the persons with whom to talk about certain matters is as important as a judicious choice of the right time, place, or occasion for conversation about them.

4. Certain matters are undiscussable and, therefore, one should avoid discussing them. The familiar maxim, *de gustibus non disputandum est*, is more often disobeyed than honored, and yet violating this rule always turns two-way talk into nothing more than an exchange of personal prejudices.

About matters concerning which individuals can differ only in their tastes or preferences, their likes and dislikes, conversation can be informative only to the extent that you may learn how the other person's taste differs from yours, or why he likes what you dislike. Such differences do not yield to argument and so there is no point in arguing about them. To do so is an utter waste of everyone's time.

In addition to likes and dislikes, concerning which one should not engage in dispute or argument, there are also personal opinions or prejudices for which no support can be given, either by an appeal to facts or by an advance of reasons. These, too, when expressed in a conversation, should simply be acknowledged for what they are and not be made the subject of discussion that aims at a meeting of minds. About such matters there can be no meeting of minds and so it is futile to argue about them.

Only about matters concerning which objective truth can be ascertained is it worthwhile to engage in argument of one sort or another for the sake of ascertaining it. The personal prejudice or unsupportable opinion that I hold may have subjective truth. It may be true for me, but not for you. If that is all there is to it, there is no point at all in my trying to defend it or in your trying to get me to change it for an opinion that is subjectively true for you, but not for me. Objective truth, in contrast, consists in that which is true, not just for you or for me, but for everyone everywhere.

5. Don't listen only to yourself. All of us have had the experience of conversation that proceeds in the following manner. Brown speaks while Jones remains silent, not listening to what Brown says, but only waiting politely for Brown to finish, at which time Jones enters the conversation with a statement of something on his mind that may have no relation whatsoever to what Brown has just said.

While Jones speaks, Brown also politely waits, but does not listen. When Jones finishes, Brown then expands on what he said earlier or talks about something else that in no way relates to what Jones has just expressed. They might just as well have been in different rooms talking to themselves, because that is the only person they have been listening to.

6. A closely related rule calls on you to listen to a question with an effort to understand it before answering it, and then with an effort to address yourself to the question in the light of your understanding of it. Many persons take questions as nothing more than signals for them to speak, uttering whatever happens to be on their mind at the moment, whether or not it has any relevance to the question that calls for their response.

If you have any sense at all that you may not understand the question you have been asked, don't try to answer it. Instead ask your interrogator to explain the question, to rephrase it in some way that makes it more intelligible to you. There is no point in trying to answer questions you do not completely understand. Keep at the task of reaching for that understanding before you attempt to answer.

7. A parallel rule, if you are on the questioning rather than the answering end of a conversation, is to ask your questions as clearly and as intelligibly as possible. Don't be a lazy questioner. Don't suppose that, because you understand the question, the way you express it makes it understandable to others. It may be necessary for you to ask the same question in a number of different ways, keeping at it until you find the one way of expressing it that really catches the mind of the other person.

8. There is still one more rule about questions in relation to good serious conversation. Some people think that they are engaging in conversation when they ask another person one question after another, receiving each answer without commenting on it, and without any connection between the questions asked in sequence. This may be a form of interrogation that is useful under certain conditions and for certain purposes, but it is not a conversation in which the interchanges of two-way talk advance significantly from one point to another.

9. Don't interrupt while someone else is speaking. Don't be so impatient to say what is on your mind that you cannot wait for the other person to finish speaking before you say it. Don't interrupt even if you think you know, from his initial remarks, what he is going to say. Give him the chance to say it.

10. Don't be rude by engaging in a side conversation while someone to whom you should be listening is talking. At the same time, don't be too polite. One should always be civil in the tone and manner of one's utterances, but

excessive politeness should not restrain one from saying what is on one's mind. If you think what you have to say may be offensive, try to phrase it in such a way that giving offense is avoided, but do not clam up when what you have to say deserves saying.

11. Recognize that anything that takes time should have a beginning, a middle, and an end. This is as true of a conversation as of a play or a symphony. Some things that take time, such as working on an assembly line, may have a beginning, middle, and end, but in an inorganic manner. Each part of the time, whether beginning, middle, or end, is like the rest. That is why the work becomes tedious. But in a play or a symphony, the beginning, middle, and end are organically related, each contributing something different to the whole. That is the way a good conversation should be organized. The more each part serves the purpose appropriate to it, the better the conversation will be.

The beginning should set the stage for the conversation by focusing on the theme—the problem, the question, the subject to be discussed. The middle, which should run for a longer time, should be devoted to exploring the problem, the question, or subject and should elicit all the differences of opinion that are relevant to it, with support for these opinions to be given by argument. The end should bring the conversation to a conclusion—a decision reached if the conversation has a practical purpose, a position agreed upon if the matter is theoretical. If agreement is beyond reach, then the conclusion may involve suspended judgment and the tabling of the matter in question for further conversation, and perhaps resolution, at a later time.

· 3 ·

An hour of good social conversation is like an hour of good amateur sport. It can be more than simply pleasurable, it can be hilariously amusing, especially if the participants observe good manners in every respect and there is equal give and take.

The topic or topics can change and develop as the conversation goes along. People may be the subject of discussion, or events, or even ideas. It is important to find topics of mutual interest to all concerned. If you see a dull glaze come over any listener's eyes, it would be advisable to change the subject, whether you are the speaker or not.

Let me put down a brief list of things to be avoided in social conversation in order to make it as enjoyable as it can be: (1) vulgarity and blasphemy; (2) ethnic jokes and slurs; (3) conceit, especially name-dropping; (4) clichés; (5) foreign words and phrases, unless perfectly pronounced and understood by all; (6) foreign clichés, such as *entre nous, ciao, savez-vous?* and the like; (7) uncommon words, especially words that are familiar only to the academic specialist or the expert; (8) the repetition of old stories or events that others have heard many times before.

There are certain subjects that need not necessarily be avoided, but should be touched on only with close friends who are really interested in what you may have to say about them: (1) one's state of health or recent surgical operations; (2) one's babies and their cute little tricks; (3) one's children and their brilliant accomplishments; (4) one's domestic pet, unless it happens to be an elephant, an alligator, or a boa constrictor.

In addition, there are a certain number of don'ts to be

observed, sensible strictures that are too frequently violated.

1. Don't digress or change the subject if the conversation is going well.

2. Don't pry into another person's private life; and don't ask questions that are too intimately personal.

3. Don't indulge in malicious gossip.

4. Don't speak about confidential matters if you really expect them not to be repeated to others.

5. Don't just chatter or repeatedly embellish your speech needlessly with social noises such as "you know," "I mean," and "as a matter of fact."

6. Don't say "Look" when you mean "Please listen."

On the positive side, there are a number of things worth recommending, such as the following:

1. Ask others about themselves; at the same time, be on guard not to talk too much about yourself.

2. Keep your voice modulated. Laugh when moved to do so, but avoid raucous laughter, and don't giggle at your own remarks.

3. Listen to whoever is speaking and make it apparent that you are listening by not letting your eyes wander or your attention be diverted.

4. If another person joins the conversation, bring him briefly up to date on what is being discussed and encourage him to join the conversation.

5. At dinner parties, break the ice by turning to the person sitting next to you and asking some question that is calculated to elicit an answer that can then become the subject of conversation. It does not make much difference

what you ask if it succeeds in getting the other person to speak.

· 4 ·

The recommendations for conducting impersonal conversation—mind-to-mind talks that are either theoretical or practical in aim—divide into two sets of rules.

One consists in the intellectual rules, rules governing the use of your mind. The other consists in emotional rules, rules for controlling one's emotions and keeping them in their place.

In practical talk that aims at persuasion, eliciting and managing to direct the emotions of others enters into the picture, as I have already pointed out in Chapter 4. Nothing more needs to be said on that subject here. I will, therefore, deal only with the managing of one's own emotions, after I have suggested the rules for using one's mind effectively in impersonal conversations.

Some of the intellectual rules I have already touched on. Some I have not mentioned before. Among the recommendations to be added are the following.

1. If you are an active participant in a conversation or discussion, your first obligation is to focus on the question to be considered. What is the problem to be solved, the issue to be settled, the subject to be explored? If the matter is complex and has a number of component elements, those engaged in the conversation would be well advised to break it up into its parts, label them, and put them in some order. This amounts to saying "Let's take this point up first, then let's turn to that, and finally we can deal with the one remaining point."

A prepared agenda for a conference or a business meeting does something like this as a guide for carrying on a discussion. But something like it can be done informally at the beginning of any conversation if the participants are wise enough to recognize that they have taken up a complex question or a subject that can be broken down into component parts.

2. Stick to the issue. Stay within the framework of the subject under consideration, either as a whole or with respect to one or another of its parts. Don't wander off and talk about something else or intrude irrelevancies into the course of the conversation.

In short, be relevant, first, last, and always. I wish I could write out a prescription for being relevant. It would provide the remedy for so many of the ills that beset our talking with one another. Being relevant simply consists in paying close attention to the point that is being talked about and saying nothing that is not significantly related to it.

Knowing what is or is not related in some significant way to the point under consideration calls for nothing more than understanding on your part. Either you have it, or you don't. If you don't there is little that can be done about it, except perhaps what most people resent and that is being told that they are off the point or irrelevant.

When two persons have the skill of talking relevantly with one another and never getting off the point, that skill resembles the skill exhibited by two persons who have long been dancing partners and know how to keep step with one another. Imagine the result if, in dancing, both persons try to lead and neither to follow. Many conversations, full of irrelevance, are precisely like that.

3. Stick to the issue or the point, but don't beat it to death. Don't stay on it forever. Keep moving on to the next point when this one has been sufficiently explored or discussed. Repetition can become deadly. Conversation can falter and fade if the persons engaged in it are unable to pass on from one point to another, if they get stalled by someone's being unable to recognize that enough has been said on a certain subject.

After a point has been settled, push on to the next one. This does not mean that you should not come back to the point if it needs reopening. But it does mean that a good conversation should be progressive. The person who has not listened attentively usually raises from the dead some point that was settled some time back. Backing and filling is one of the fatal diseases of conversation.

4. Individuals not only bring unacknowledged assumptions to a conversation in which they are engaged, they also take part in it without knowing what their blind spots are—matters concerning which they lack understanding and have difficulty in attaining. Like unacknowledged assumptions, blind spots can ruin a conversation or at least prevent the minds engaged in it from really meeting.

What's to be done to overcome these obstacles? My only recommendation here is that you should be on the alert to recognize when you are failing to understand something and press for help in understanding it. You should be aware that you have certain preconceptions and assumptions, and try to dredge them up from the recesses of your mind and lay them on the table for everyone to examine.

Since few conversations begin at the beginning and different things are taken for granted by the persons talking with one another, the rule might better be stated as follows. Ask your companions to grant the assumptions you wish to make, and state your own assumptions when it comes their turn to ask you for them.

We frequently suspect that the other person is making assumptions, though precisely what they are we seldom know. We, too, infrequently recognize that we ourselves are also making assumptions. The best cure is for everyone to try to make his own assumptions explicit and beg the others to accept them pro tem.

If this is not done, then sooner or later somebody says, "Wait a minute, Joe. What makes you think that we all agree that men are created equal?"

Sometimes the assumptions declared can themselves be made the subject of the argument, but when that is not possible, because it would take too long or go too far back, the assumption should be granted for the sake of going forward with the discussion. It can then proceed in a hypothetical manner by noting what consequences follow on the supposition that a certain assumption is true.

The argument can move forward either by dealing with pros and cons about the assumption itself or about what follows from supposing it to be correct. I can accept your assumption as something to take for granted for the moment, and still think you have reached a wrong conclusion from it.

5. Avoid the most obvious fallacies. Never argue about facts; look them up if you wish to settle a difference of opinion about them.

Never cite authorities as if the citation of them were conclusive. Even if you don't make that mistake, keep the mention of authorities out of the talk unless mentioning them really makes a contribution to what is being said. That happens only when the authority is not simply named as supporting what you yourself are trying to say, but when a significant statement by the authority can be accurately quoted and when quoting it genuinely adds something to what you yourself have already said.

If George Washington was against entangling alliances or a third term in the office of the President, it may be worth mentioning. What great or wise men have said deserves our consideration. But great and wise men have sometimes made mistakes, just like the rest of us. Even when they were right about a certain point centuries ago, they may be wrong today. Authorities may support your position, but only sound reasons and the weight of the evidence can make it acceptable to others.

Related to the mistake of citing authorities as conclusive is the even worse mistake of calling attention to the kind of person with whom someone who disagrees with you is aligned. You suppose everyone will recognize that the kind of person you are referring to is one of ill repute. This is arguing ad hominem. It is attacking persons rather than attacking the point being considered. It is a vicious form of irrelevance.

Never make irrelevant references to the other person's grandmother, his nationality, his business or political associates, his occupation, or his personal habits. All such tactics are instances of the fallacious ad hominem argument. The most exasperating form of this fallacy is the bedfellow argument. You say to someone, "So you agree with Hitler," as if this suffices to discredit the point he is trying to make. Hitler may be in ill repute with everyone present, but that does not mean he is necessarily wrong about everything.

In certain types of practical conversations that aim at reaching a decision, especially in business matters or in politics, it may be necessary to take a vote if it is foreordained that the matter is to be decided by the weight of the majority. Taking a vote is not necessary if the leader of a group, in business or in politics, regards the opinions of his associates as advisory rather than decisive. Then he decides, sometimes against the majority, sometimes with it. But taking a vote is never necessary and always undesirable when the conversation does not lead to action and no decision need be made.

When the conversation is theoretical rather than practical, when it is concerned with getting at the truth about a certain matter, then taking a vote should never be regarded as settling the question in issue. Here the majority can very easily be wrong. Everyone present may disagree with you and you may still be right. You can also be wrong even if the majority agrees with you. Being satisfied with such agreement may delude you into closing your mind to further argument. Counting noses settles nothing except the number of ayes and nays.

Beware of examples. They often prove too much or too little and they are seldom perfectly relevant. The fact that you saw a roadway worker leaning on a shovel and staring into space hardly proves that all roadway workers are lazy or that the indolence of labor is the cause of reduced productivity. The conversation starts going around in circles when, after you have cited an example, all the others in the room follow suit and introduce examples in support of what they are saying.

Examples can be useful, but only to illustrate what you are saying, never to prove it. They should be well chosen for the purpose of making a general statement of your point more intelligible. Many persons have difficulty in dealing with generalizations, especially when these are stated at a high level of abstraction. A concrete example offered to illustrate something stated abstractly helps them to understand what is being said.

If you don't understand what others are saying, it is not only proper but also prudent for you to ask them to give you an example of the point. If they cannot do this to your satisfaction, it may be fair to suspect that they themselves do not fully understand what they are trying to say.

Examples should be treated like assumptions. Just as assumptions should be allowed to exert whatever force they have only with everyone's explicit acknowledgment and consent, so examples should stand only if everyone sees their relevance and is aware that they are being used to illustrate a point, not to prove it.

I turn now to the rules that concern controlling emotions in the course of a conversation in which they are out of place because it is an impersonal talk either about theoretical matters or important practical problems.

The first recommendation here is to catch yourself or the other person getting angry. The signs that this is happening are many and various: you or he start to shout; you or he become repetitious, raising your voice with each reiteration of the point; you or he become overpositive, expressing this by pounding the table or by other forms of gesturing; you or he indulge in sarcasm, in teasing, in baiting, or in getting the other's argument laughed at; or either of you resorts to the kind of irrelevant ad hominems mentioned above.

If you indulge in sarcasm, or try to get the laugh on your opponent, or bait him by harping on unimportant mistakes he has made, or argue ad hominem, you will goad your opponent into losing his temper also. If he resists all your attacks and remains cool, he will probably enrage you further. When a discussion reaches this point, it becomes a battle of nit-picking and of low blows. It ceases to be a sensible or significant conversation worth continuing.

Our emotions play an important role in everything we do and say, but they do not help us to talk sense or to converse in a profitable and pleasurable manner. When you find yourself getting annoyed, angry, or overexcited in the course of an argument, leave the room and give yourself time to cool off.

If another member of the group gets fighting mad, you have only two alternatives. Try to soothe him or placate him in a friendly way. If that does not work, change the subject for a while. He is probably just as nice as you are, but something happened to hit him in a tender spot. The barkeeper's advice, "If you want to fight, go outside to do it," should be followed. Suspend the conversation when it ceases to be an impersonal mind-to-mind talk and turns into a passionate conflict.

Do not allow an impersonal discussion to become a personal quarrel. Argument is not aggression. There is no point at all in trying to win an argument simply by putting your opponent down or beating him up.

Be aware of the results of emotional disorder on your own part. It will lead you to suppress points that you really do see but which weaken your case, because you do not want to give in to your opponent. For purely emotional reasons, you find such acquiescence distasteful.

You may also, for purely emotional reasons, stubbornly refuse to concede that you are in the wrong when you really know that you are. There is certainly no point in winning an argument for personal or emotional reasons that impel you to try to get the better of the other person when your mind either knows now or will recognize later that he was right and you were wrong.

CHAPTER **XII**

The Meeting of Minds

· I ·

The meeting of two minds may consist in their understanding of one another while still in disagreement or it may consist in their coming into agreement as a result of their understanding one another.

All impersonal conversations, whether theoretical or practical in aim, should strive to conclude with a meeting of minds in one or the other form in which that can be achieved.

Practical conversations are often unsuccessful because misunderstanding prevents them from reaching a decision. Even with sufficient understanding present, disagreement can block the way to action.

Theoretical conversations that engage persons in the pursuit of objective truth about a certain matter may not end with a meeting of minds but may still be profitable for all concerned. The pursuit of objective truth is a long, arduous, and difficult enterprise. A good conversation may help the individuals engaged in it to make some advance toward their goal, but it will seldom if ever enable them to reach it with finality and incorrigibility.

About any matter of objective truth, the ultimate goal is universal agreement, but about certain matters of this sort, it may take until the end of time to achieve it. The pursuit of truth has many stages. At each stage some progress may be made and yet still fall short of the goal aimed at.

Individuals may engage in conversation after conversation about a certain subject, the truth about which concerns them. Each of these conversations may constitute a progressive stage in their pursuit of the truth. The fact that none achieves a state of mutual understanding and complete agreement that is final, conclusive, and incorrigible does not render any of them unprofitable if some advance toward the goal is made.

With these general observations noted and heeded, let us consider how persons engaged in such conversations or discussions should proceed with regard to achieving understanding and agreement, at least pro tem, if not for all time.

· 2 ·

The first rule to be followed is this. Do not disagree— or, for that matter, do not agree—with anyone else unless you are sure you understand the position the other person is taking. To disagree before you understand is impertinent. To agree is inane.

To make sure that you understand, before you disagree or agree, exercise the courtesy of asking the other person the following question: "Do I understand you to say that . . . ?" Fill in the blank by phrasing in your own words what you think you hear the other person saying. He may respond to this by saying to you, "No, that is not what I said or not what I meant. My position is as follows." Then, after the other person has restated his position for you, you should once again try to state in your own words what you have understood the other to say. If the other still dissents from your interpretation, you must continue with this question and answer procedure until the other tells you that you have at last caught the point, that you understand him precisely as he wishes to be understood. Only then do you have the grounds indispensable for intelligent and reasonable disagreement or agreement.

This procedure is time consuming. It requires patience and persistence. Most people anxious to get on with the discussion bypass it. They are willing to risk being impertinent or inane by disagreeing or agreeing with what they do not understand. They are satisfied with merely apparent disagreements or agreements, instead of seeking a genuine meeting of minds.

Real as opposed to apparent agreement occurs when two persons, concerned with a certain question to be answered, understand that question in exactly the same way yet give incompatible answers to the question on which their minds meet in mutual understanding.

Apparent as opposed to real disagreement occurs when two persons, concerned with a certain question, do not understand that question in exactly the same way. When their minds have not met in mutual understanding of the question, the incompatible answers they give to it constitute a difference of opinion that is not a genuine disagreement, even though it may appear to be such. Real disagreement occurs only when, with their minds meeting in mutual understanding of the question, they then give incompatible answers to it.

When two persons find themselves in real disagreement,

a meeting of minds about that very disagreement still remains to be achieved. It takes the form of understanding their disagreement. To achieve this, each must forsake partisanship with regard to his own position, and substitute for it a kind of impartiality with respect to the position taken by the other person. What I mean by an attitude of impartiality is trying to understand why the other individual holds the view he does. Each person should not only be able to state the position of the other in a manner that the other approves, he should also be able to state the other person's reasons for holding that view.

One thus sympathetically entertains a position with which one still does not agree. Thereby one at least fully understands the view not agreed to. Understanding with disagreement—fully understood disagreement—constitutes a minimal meeting of minds. A more complete meeting of minds consists in understanding with agreement—fully understood agreement.

All of us should be aware of the moral obligation that the pursuit of objective truth imposes upon us. If we find ourselves in real disagreement with others, we should be tireless in our effort to resolve that disagreement. We should never desist from trying to overcome it and reach agreement.

If one conversation does not succeed in doing this, then we should try again at some other time, and we should keep on trying no matter how protracted and difficult the process may be. We should never discontinue the argument as profitless.

To do so is to abandon the pursuit of truth and to treat the matter in question as if it belonged to the sphere of taste. That means treating it as if the disagreement were a conflict between purely personal and unsupportable opinions, purely subjective prejudices or preferences, about which agreement should not be sought and about which one should not engage in argument.

If you find yourself in genuine disagreement with the position taken by another, you should be able to explain the grounds of your disagreement, by saying one or more of the following things.

1. "I think you hold that position because you are uninformed about certain facts or reasons that have a critical bearing on it." Then be prepared to point out the information you think the other lacks and which, if possessed, would result in a change of mind.

2. "I think you hold that position because you are misinformed about matters that are critically relevant." Then be prepared to indicate the mistakes the other has made, which, if corrected, would lead the other to abandon the position taken.

3. "I think you are sufficiently well informed and have a firm grasp of the evidence and reasons that support your position, but you have drawn the wrong conclusions from your premises because you have made mistakes in reasoning. You have made fallacious inferences." Then be ready to point out those logical errors which, if corrected, would bring the other person to a different conclusion.

4. "I think you have made none of the foregoing errors and that you have proceeded by sound reasoning from adequate grounds for the conclusion you have reached, but I also think that your thinking about the subject is incomplete. You should have gone further than you did and reached other conclusions that somewhat alter or qualify the one you did reach." Then be able to point out what

these other conclusions are and how they alter or qualify the position taken by the person with whom you disagree.

· 3 ·

Mind-to-mind talks that are practical in character, where a decision must be reached for the sake of action, are unprofitable unless there is a meeting of the minds in understood agreement or understood disagreement.

Here, because of the practical urgency that surrounds the attempt to solve practical problems by discussion, the pursuit of truth cannot be interminable. A decision may sometimes have to be made with something less than a meeting of minds upon the part of all concerned. Dissenting opinions may have to be recorded for whatever benefit they confer upon future attempts to solve similar problems, as is the case in the rendering of judicial decisions by a majority vote, accompanied by the upholding and dissenting views concerning the decision laid down.

With this in mind, it is important to recognize that thinking and talking about practical problems can and should occur at three different levels. The highest level—the one most remote from a practical decision and the action to follow—is concerned with the universal principles applicable to the problem under consideration. About such principles, it should always be possible to achieve a meeting of minds. They have the kind of objective truth that is ascertainable. That being the case, agreement should also be attainable.

At the next level down are the general rules or policies that represent the application of universal principles to different sets of contingent circumstances, varying with time and place. On this level, reasonable men can disagree and their disagreement may be irresolvable. The same holds for the third and lowest level, where general rules and policies are applied to particular cases. Here, in the process of casuistry, it is even more to be expected that reasonable persons may disagree.

For example, agreement should be attainable about the universal principles of justice, even though there may be a long-standing controversy about the nature or principles of justice. Let us suppose, for the moment, that two persons discussing a practical problem, the solution of which involves the principles of justice, are in complete agreement about them. Their meeting of minds on this level does not preclude them from disagreeing subsequently when they move to a lower level and discuss what rules or policies should be adopted in the application of the agreed upon principles to the contingent circumstances that create the problem they are considering.

Even less does it preclude their disagreement when they move to the lowest level and, with some measure of agreement about the rules or policies to be adopted, try to apply them casuistically to reach a decision about what should be done here and now in this particular case. Their disagreement here will probably stem from different estimates of the probable consequences or different judgments about the circumstances that should be taken into account.

One mistake that many people make, which should be strenuously avoided, is thinking that their agreement about the universal principles is of no practical importance because it does not inevitably lead to agreement about the general rules or policies to be adopted or about the decision that should result from trying to apply such general rules or policies to particular cases.

Their formulation of the conflicting general rules or policies to be adopted was grounded on their understanding and agreement about the universal principles. Their difference of opinion about these, as well as about their application to a particular case or problem, would not be reasonable if it were not grounded in their agreement about the universal principles.

They should not, therefore, abandon their agreement about the universal principles or think it of no practical significance because it does not inexorably lead them to further agreement at the lower level of general rules or policies or at the still lower level of particular decisions.

· 4 ·

Having said that understood disagreement is a great good to be achieved, and that understood agreement is an even greater good, I must add a few final, cautionary remarks about the meeting of minds as the ultimate desideratum of all our impersonal conversations, both theoretical and practical.

First of all, let me say that we should not be satisfied with too little, because human beings, insofar as they are rational, should strive to attain the desired goal. They should not, through sloth or immoderate skepticism about objective truth and its pursuit, be tempted to avoid the difficulties involved in following the rules or recommendations for making conversation or discussion as good as it can be.

At the same time, we should not expect too much. Human beings—creatures of passion as well as of intellect, with minds that are often clouded by their feelings, and with all the other limitations to which their fallible minds are subject—must be satisfied with some measure of approximation to the ideal and not inordinately seek its complete realization, at least not at any given time or place.

We can never completely master our emotions and should not expect to, even when managing them properly is highly desirable. We can never completely get out of ourselves and into the other person's shoes and see things as he or she sees them. Partisanship and partiality can never be completely replaced by the impartial attitude that enables one to take the other person's position in the same way that he or she holds it.

If a particular conversation ends with understood agreement about a matter of objective truth, we should not regard that as finishing the matter. More remains to be done in an effort to understand the presuppositions and implications of the agreement reached. If it ends with understood disagreement, more also remains to be done.

The cautionary remark that is relevant here consists in the advice that there is another time and place for pushing matters further. Stop for the time being and return to the subject on another day. This is especially sound advice if a conversation reaches an impasse, as many conversations do when their duration is too limited.

Finally, let me say that good conversation calls for an exercise of moral virtue. It requires the fortitude needed to take the pains necessary to make it good. It requires the temperance needed for a moderation of one's passions. Above all, it requires the justice needed to give the other person his due.

CHAPTER XIII

Seminars: Teaching and Learning by Discussion

· I ·

Lectures and other forms of instructive speech are teaching by telling. This is didactic teaching. The seminar is different. It is teaching by asking and by a discussion conducted through questions asked and answered and with answers often disputed. This is Socratic teaching.

There is a third form of teaching, which is coaching. This is indispensable for the development of intellectual skills as much as it is for athletic and bodily skills. The skills of reading and writing, of speaking and listening, and of observing, calculating, measuring, and estimating, cannot be inculcated by means of didactic instruction. Skilled habits can be formed only through practise under supervision by a coach who corrects wrong moves and requires that right ones be made.

The three kinds of teaching—didactic, Socratic, and coaching—are correlated with three kinds of learning. The acquisition of organized knowledge in basic fields of subject matter is the kind of learning that is aided by didactic teaching—teaching by telling, lectures, and textbooks. The development of all the intellectual skills is the kind of learning that requires coaching. The third form of teaching—the Socratic method of teaching by asking and by discussion—facilitates the kind of learning that is an enlargement of the understanding of basic ideas and values.

This tripartite distinction of kinds of teaching and kinds of learning, diagrammed on the opposite page, is the focal point of *The Paideia Proposal: An Educational Manifesto*, which was published last year. While I was nominally the author of that book, it expressed the views agreed upon by my associates in an effort to propose a much needed radical reform of basic schooling in the United States.

Among other things, the reform calls for the restoration of coaching in our schools. This has almost disappeared from the first twelve years of schooling. The reform also calls for the introduction of Socratic teaching, the seminar method of teaching. Seminars, in which the teaching proceeds by asking and discussion, are, with very few exceptions, not present at all during the first twelve years of schooling. Nor are they present in any but a few colleges.

Their absence leaves a large and deplorable gap in the development of the growing mind. From long experience with it, I also know that the seminar kind of teaching and learning makes the most fruitful contribution to the continued growth of the mature mind.

· 2 ·

I have been conducting seminars for sixty years now, with students in high schools and colleges and with adults who have engaged in the reading and discussion of great books or who have been participants in the Aspen Executive Seminars.

Long experience has convinced me that seminar teach-

	COLUMN ONE	COLUMN TWO	COLUMN THREE
Goals	ACQUISITION OF ORGANIZED KNOWLEDGE	DEVELOPMENT OF INTELLECTUAL SKILLS – SKILLS OF LEARNING	ENLARGED UNDERSTANDING OF IDEAS AND VALUES
	by means of	by means of	by means of
Means	DIDACTIC INSTRUCTION LECTURES AND RESPONSES TEXTBOOKS AND OTHER AIDS	COACHING, EXERCISES, AND SUPERVISED PRACTICE	MAIEUTIC OR SOCRATIC QUESTIONING AND ACTIVE PARTICIPATION
	in three areas of subject-matter	in the operations of	in the
Areas Operations and Activities	LANGUAGE, LITERATURE, AND THE FINE ARTS MATHEMATICS AND NATURAL SCIENCE HISTORY, GEOGRAPHY, AND SOCIAL STUDIES	READING, WRITING, SPEAKING, LISTENING CALCULATING, PROBLEM- SOLVING OBSERVING, MEASURING, ESTIMATING EXERCISING CRITICAL JUDGMENT	DISCUSSION OF BOOKS (NOT TEXTBOOKS) AND OTHER WORKS OF ART AND INVOLVEMENT IN ARTISTIC ACTIVITIES e.g., MUSIC, DRAMA, VISUAL ARTS

THE THREE COLUMNS DO NOT CORRESPOND TO SEPARATE COURSES, NOR IS ONE KIND OF TEACHING AND LEARNING NECESSARILY CONFINED TO ANY ONE CLASS ing, on the Greek or Socratic model, not the German one, belongs not only in the colleges but should be carried on also in the high schools, where students have proved every bit as able to profit from seminars that I have conducted as have their college counterparts—have shown themselves even better participants in some ways.

I am further convinced that the seminar method is appropriate for the continued learning of adults, especially the improvement of their understanding of basic ideas and issues. That should begin, however, and can, when they are much younger.

In the past few years, when the Paideia Group was at work formulating its proposals for the reform of basic schooling in the United States, I have conducted seminars at Aspen for young people ranging in age from ten to eighteen. At the invitation of various school systems, I have gone around the country demonstrating the Socratic method of teaching by conducting seminars for high school students, to be observed by teachers in those school systems. From this most recent experience, I have been fully persuaded of the necessity to introduce this kind of teaching and learning at all levels of basic schooling.

Students who have participated in these seminars have told me, in the most poignant terms, that this was their first experience of being asked to think about ideas and issues, their first experience in expressing and defending their views about important subjects.

On occasion after occasion, it has been patently obvious that their prior schooling had not given them any preparation for the kind of learning that a seminar provides. They have not been prepared to think for themselves in answering questions about important ideas, nor prepared to speak clearly and coherently as well as to listen well.

Ideas, issues, values—these constitute the ideal subject matter for seminars. Reading great books or selections from them provides the substance for discussion, but other well chosen reading materials are also useful for the purpose, as in the Aspen Executive Seminars.

It is even possible to conduct seminars by the questioning method in which no reading materials at all are used. Instead, the participants can be asked to state what understanding they have of a fundamental idea, such as progress, or liberty, or justice. When their answers are laid on the table and examined by further questioning, the discussion proceeds to explore the idea from every angle and to deal with the issues raised by conflicting views about its significance.

It would take too many pages to report my experience with the Aspen Executive Seminars over the last thirty years. From this experience I have learned a great deal about the ideas there discussed—more, perhaps, than any of the other participants involved.

Instead, for the benefit of the readers of this book, I have put into Appendix II a speech that I delivered at the Aspen Institute in 1972. It not only indicates the sequence of readings used in the seminars, but also summarizes what I and the other participants have learned as a result of our discussion of the ideas treated in those readings.

In the remainder of this chapter, I am going to try to distill from my seminar teaching experiences, under a wide variety of circumstances and with a wide variety of groups, the suggestions and recommendations I am able to formulate concerning the conduct of such seminars.

All the rules and recommendations set forth in the two preceding chapters, intended to provide guidance for making conversations of every sort more profitable and pleasurable, apply, of course, to the kind of conversation that takes place in a seminar. Seminar discussion is simply that special kind of conversation or two-way talk in which a moderator, or sometimes a pair of moderators, exercises some control over the course of the conversation and the direction it takes from beginning to end.

The additional rules or recommendations that may be helpful mainly concern how moderators should play their special part in these proceedings and how the participants should try to respond in ways that make the seminars fruitful.

· 3 ·

Let me begin by saying what seminar teaching by questioning and discussion is not.

It is not a quiz session in which a teacher asks Yes or No questions and says right or wrong to the answers.

It is not a lecture in disguise in which the teacher asks questions and, after a brief pause or after listening to one or two unsatisfactory responses, then proceeds to answer his own questions at length, thus in effect giving a lecture that is punctuated by the questions asked.

It is not a glorified "bull session" in which everyone feels equally free to express opinions on the level of personal prejudices or to recount experiences that the narrator of them regards as highly significant of something or other.

None of the foregoing counterfeits of the seminar provides the kind of learning that a seminar should afford when it is properly conducted by questions and answers and by the discussion of their significance. For the purpose of such learning, discussable subject matter is required—ideally, basic ideas, issues, or values proposed by the moderator either on the basis of reading done or without such reading.

There are other prerequisites. One is duration. A good seminar needs sufficient time for its development—at least an hour and a half, more often two hours or more. The canonical fifty-minute classroom session is much too short a duration for the development of the discussion that should take place.

A second prerequisite is the furniture of the room in which the seminar is to occur. It should have a hollow square table; or, even better, the kind of large hexagonal table used in Aspen, around which the participants sit, able to face one another as they talk. The seminar room should be the very antithesis of the ordinary classroom or lecture hall, in which the teacher or lecturer stands in front of auditors who sit in row after row to listen to what he has to say. That kind of room may be ideal for uninterrupted speech and silent listening, but it is the very opposite for good two-way talk in which everyone is both a speaker and a listener.

A third prerequisite is the state of mind that the participants bring to the seminar. It should be both open and docile.

All the participants, including the moderator, should be prepared to change their minds as a result of the discussion in which they engage. They should be open to views that are new to them. They should be docile in considering such new views, neither stubbornly resistant to something they have never thought of before nor passively submissive.

The virtue of docility (i.e., of teachability), which is the cardinal virtue in all forms of learning, should predispose them to examine new views before they adopt or reject them and also to be openly receptive of them for the sake of examining them. Persons who are stubbornly contentious or disputatious, who argue for the sake of argument, not for the sake of learning, as well as persons who are too submissive or acquiescent and do not exercise their minds critically, lack docility.

· 4 ·

The task of the moderator is threefold: (1) to ask a series of questions that control the discussion and give it direction; (2) to examine the answers by trying to evoke the reasons for them or the implications they have; and (3) to engage the participants in two-way talk with one another when the views they have advanced appear to be in conflict. The conversation that then ensues among the participants themselves, and sometimes with the moderator involved in it, is the very heart of a good seminar.

In order to perform the second and third of these tasks well, the moderator must be as active in listening as in questioning. From my long experience with seminars, I know this to be the moderator's most important obligation and the one most difficult to discharge well.

The energy required to listen to each and every one of the twenty or twenty-five participants in a seminar is very tiring, but the moderator must strive to overcome fatigue and continue to listen actively throughout the seminar. It is quite easy to give two or three good lectures in a single day, but I seriously doubt that anyone has enough energy to conduct more than one good seminar between sunrise and sunset.

Energetic effort on the moderator's part is also required for questioning. He is not doing his part if he just sits back as a chairman of the meeting and invites the participants to take turns speaking, calling on them in the order in which they have indicated their acceptance of that invitation. That may maintain order by preventing everyone from speaking at once, but it certainly does not produce the kind of learning that a seminar is intended to stimulate. Only Socratic questioning can do that.

That kind of learning stems ultimately from the questions the moderator asks. They should be questions that raise issues; questions that raise further questions when first answers are given to them; questions that can seldom be answered simply by Yes or No; hypothetical questions that present suppositions the implications or consequences of which are to be examined; questions that are complex and have many related parts, to be taken up in an orderly manner.

Above all, the moderator must make sure that the questions he asks are listened to and understood, that they are not merely taken as signals for the person who is queried to respond by saying whatever is on his or her mind, whether or not it is a relevant answer to the question asked.

The moderator should be so insistent upon an understanding of his questions that he should be prepared to ask the same questions over and over again in different phrasings of it and with different examples to illuminate it. The participants should be warned that they are not to answer a question until they are relatively sure that they understand it. If not, they should persist in getting the moderator to rephrase the question.

All this requires intense activity and great expenditure of energy on the part of both moderators and participants. It should go without saying that it also calls upon both moderators and participants to listen intently and to speak as clearly as possible. Neither should put up with half-minded listening or with garbled, incoherent speech. Neither should rest content with statements that appear to be generally acceptable without also seeking for the reasons that underlie them or the consequences that flow from their truth.

· 5 ·

I have just described what is involved in the conduct of seminars by the Socratic method of questioning without paying attention to what kind of seminar it is. One kind of seminar is that in which the participants are all adults, such as the Aspen Executive Seminars, in which the moderator may not be a professional teacher. Quite different are seminars in schools and colleges, in which the moderator is a professional teacher and a difference in age and maturity exists between the moderator and the younger participants.

In the former case, the seminar serves the purpose of continued learning by mature persons, long after they have left school. In the latter case, it is an essential ingredient in schooling, which is at best a stage of learning that should prepare for continued learning in the mature years of adult life. Without this no one can expect to become an educated person no matter how much or how good the schooling he had while immature.

When members of the teaching profession are called upon to moderate seminars in schools, they soon realize that Socratic teaching is utterly different from the kind of didactic teaching they are so used to doing, which is perhaps the only kind of teaching they have ever done.

Didactic teaching puts them in the position of knowing

more than their students. Unless they do, they are not thought by themselves or anyone to be competent teachers. They have knowledge that the students should acquire. The lectures they give are intended to transmit that knowledge from the mind of the teacher to the minds of the students.

That is not the way Socratic teaching works in seminars. There the teacher as moderator should simply be a more competent learner than the student, more competent in the effort to achieve an understanding of whatever materials are to be discussed, and more competent to do this by means of carrying on an intelligent conversation or discussion.

The teacher, as leader of a discussion, should *not* regard his competence as consisting in knowing all the right answers to the questions that should be asked and explored. To many of the questions that should be asked, there is no one right answer, but many answers that compete for attention, understanding, or judgment. The discussion leader's competence should, therefore, consist of an awareness of the important questions that have a range of answers deserving consideration and demanding judgment.

When news of *The Paideia Proposal* circulated before the publication of the book, I was asked by *The American School Board Journal* to write an article about my experience in conducting seminars with young people. I was asked also to offer such advice as I could give about how to put this kind of teaching and learning into every school in this country, at least from the seventh grade on.

In Appendix III, I have placed excerpts from the article I wrote—the portions of it that state my recommendations for setting such seminars up and conducting them.

PART FIVE
Epilogue

CHAPTER **XIV**

Conversation in Human Life

· I ·

Of all the things that human beings do, conversing with one another is the most characteristically human. It may be in the long run the only human activity the performance of which will ultimately preserve the radical distinction between humans and brutes and between men and machines.

In this century, chimpanzees have been trained by humans to use sign language with severely limited vocabularies. To those whose fanciful interpretation of the phenomena remains uncritical, the chimps give an appearance of making statements and of responding to human questions. Be that as it may, chimpanzees do not talk with one another, and in a state of nature they do not talk at all. Their communication in the wild, as with all the other higher mammals, including bottle-nosed dolphins, is by means of signals, not by means of signs that have reference to either perceptual objects or objects of thought.

The point is not that man is the only animal that communicates with his kind. Some form of communication occurs among all social animals. The point lies rather in the

181]

precise kind of communication that takes place. Human communication in two-way talk can achieve a meeting of minds, a sharing of understandings and thoughts, of feelings and wishes.

Shared thoughts and feelings, understood agreements and disagreements, make humans the only animals that genuinely *commune* with one another. Even though they signal their emotions or impulses to one another, other animals remain shut out from each other. They do not commune with one another when they communicate. The human community would not exist without such communion, which would not exist without human conversation.

This century has also seen the production of computer-like machines that are eulogistically referred to as artificial-intelligence machines. Their inventors and exponents claim for them that they will soon be able to do everything that the mind enables human beings to do. Their claim goes further than predicting that these machines will someday simulate characteristically human performances of all sorts, such as reading and writing, listening and speaking, as well as calculating, problem solving, and decision making. It predicts that the machine performance of these operations will be indistinguishable from the human performance of them.

Three centuries ago, a famous French philosopher, René Descartes, countered this prediction by asserting that there would always remain at least one thing that would separate the performance of machines from that of human beings. This one thing, which machines would never be able to simulate so successfully that machine and human performance would be indistinguishable, Descartes said, was conversation. For him that was the acid test of the radical difference in kind between humans and brutes as well as between men and machines.

In Part V of his *Discourse on Method*, Descartes conceded that intricate machines might be constructed to simulate successfully the performance of other animals—brutes by virtue of their lack of intellect, reason, or the power of conceptual thought. If there were machines possessing the organs and outward form of a monkey or some other animal without reason, Descartes agreed that "we would not have any means of ascertaining that they were not of the same nature as those animals." And in another place he wrote:

It is a very remarkable fact that there are none so depraved or stupid, without even excepting idiots, that they cannot arrange different words together, forming of them a statement by which they can make known their thoughts; while, on the other hand, there is no other animal, however perfect and fortunately circumstanced it may be, which can do the same. . . .

This does not merely show that the brutes have less reason than men, but that they have none at all, since it is clear that very little is required in order to be able to talk. . . .

A central thesis in the philosophy of Descartes was that *matter cannot think*. It was, therefore, quite consonant with the whole tenor of his thought to use machines—purely material mechanisms—as a challenge to his materialistic opponents. Here is the passage in which he hurls that challenge at them. I quote only the first part of it.

If there were machines which bore a resemblance to our body and imitated our actions so far as it was morally [i.e., practically] possible to do so, we should always have two very certain tests by which to recognize that, for all that, they were not real men.

The first is that they could never use speech or other signs as we do when placing our thought on record for the benefit of others. For we can easily understand a machine's being constituted so that it can utter words, and even emit some responses to action on it of a corporeal kind, which brings about a change in its organs; for instance, if it is touched in a particular part, it may ask what we wish to say to it; if in another part, it may exclaim that it is being hurt and so on. But it [could] never happen that it [would] arrange its speech in various ways, in order to reply appropriately to everything that may be said in its presence, as even the lowest type of man can do.

What Descartes is here saying, as I understand it, stresses the almost infinite flexibility and variety of human conversation. If over a long period of time two human beings were continuously engaged in two-way talk with one another, interrupted only by brief periods of sleep, it would be impossible to predict with certainty what turns such conversation would take, what interchanges would occur, what questions would be asked, what answers would be given.

It is precisely this unpredictability that makes human conversation something that programmed machinery will never be able to simulate in a manner that renders it indistinguishable from human performance. The twentieth-century revision of Descartes's dictum, that matter cannot think, is as follows: all the wizardry of man's technology will never be able to shape matter into truly thinking machines.

I attempted to explain why this is so in the speech that I have placed in Appendix I. I think I have there demonstrated that machines will never—never in the whole of future time—be able to engage in anything like human conversation. Instead of repeating the argument here, I refer the reader to Appendix I for that demonstration.

Readers persuaded by my argument will share my conclusion that only human minds, intellects with the power of conceptual thought, can engage in conversation with one another. Two-way talk that can end in a meeting of minds will always remain the irrefutable evidence that man is radically different in kind from brute animals and artificial intelligence machines.

· 2 ·

The communion that can be achieved by human conversation is of great significance for our private lives. It unites the members of a family—husbands and wives, parents and children. It is the spiritual parallel of the physical union by which lovers try to become one.

Please note that I did not say "the communion *achieved* by human conversation." I said rather "the communion that *can be achieved* by human conversation." Human beings sometimes—in fact, too often—fail to achieve it by their failures as speakers and listeners in two-way talk, especially in personal heart-to-heart talks.

When they fail, the sexual bond that unites husband and wife, unaccompanied by spiritual communion, usually fails to preserve their marriage. Divorce as frequently results from the failure to communicate intimately in heart-to-heart talks as it does from the weakening of sexual attraction.

One kind of intercourse without the other kind of interchange between spouses is less than completely human. Nor is it enough for them to be able to converse intimately about personal or emotional matters. A marriage not enlivened by sustained conversations about a wide variety of subjects, from which there results a meeting of minds in understood agreements or disagreements, has vacuums or voids in it that need to be filled to give it vitality.

Something similar can be said about the relation of parents and children. The so-called generation gap is just such a void or vacuum created by failures in communication between the young, especially adolescents, and their parents. The most obvious sign that the barrier that adolescence erects between them and their parents has been overcome lies in the fact that they are once again able to talk freely and frankly with their parents. Such communion reunites them after adolescence has separated them. When that does not happen, a permanent estrangement prevails in its place.

The broken home, the split-up family, whether it occurs through the divorce of husband and wife or an estrangement between parents and children, testifies that conversation has completely deteriorated, if it ever truly existed.

Outside the bonds of family life, friends and lovers face the same ultimate alternatives. Their friendship and love endure as a genuine communion only as long as they are both able, and also persistent in their effort, to engage in profitable and pleasurable conversation with one another.

Aristotle defined the highest form of friendship as that which involves the communion of persons of like character, two persons alike in their moral virtue. I would add that it also involves the existence of intellectual communion through conversation that achieves a meeting of minds.

However effective human conversation may be in achieving the communion of hearts and minds, it can never be so perfect that the solitariness of the individual is ever completely overcome. All of us are somewhat imprisoned in the solitude of our own minds and hearts. There always remain thoughts and feelings that we never do succeed in sharing completely with others.

We may never be as completely locked out from one another as other animals are, but we also never fully overcome the barriers to communion. We never achieve on earth that perfection of community which is attributed by theologians to the communion of saints and the company of angels in heaven.

· 3 ·

Turning now from our private lives to our dealings with one another in business and in politics, the contribution made by good conversation in both contexts is amply clear.

Few business enterprises are conducted without frequent and lengthy conferences, often too frequent and too protracted as well as too wasteful of time and energy when they are measured by the benefits they confer.

The agenda laid down are often poorly constructed. The discussion often wanders from the point at issue. The interchanges often exhibit inattention and failure to listen well enough to produce relevant responses to what others have said, and what others have said may often be too poorly expressed to elicit or deserve careful listening. The discussion too often fails to move on from point to point, making progress toward the decision aimed at.

When a later business conference succeeds an earlier one because there has been no meeting of minds at the earlier one (no understood agreement or disagreement about the solution of a practical problem from which decisive action should ensue), the succeeding conference too often fails to begin with an adequate summary of what has already been covered. It too often consists largely in repetitious talk instead of talk that moves forward from ground already covered.

Let me tell one autobiographical story that illustrates the importance of improving business conferences. In the late thirties, when I felt frustrated by the impediments to the educational reforms that Hutchins and I were advocating at the University of Chicago, I considered leaving the university and accepting a job at R. H. Macy and Company in New York.

I was offered a salary six times my compensation as a professor. When I asked Percy Strauss, then Chairman of the Board of that corporation, what title the job carried, I was told that I would become Vice-President in charge of Department X. When I then inquired what my duties would be, I was told that they would consist in thinking about every aspect of R. H. Macy's business.

That seemed a little vague to me. I pressed Mr. Strauss for a more concrete answer. Instead of giving it to me, he asked me what I thought I could do for the corporation that would merit the salary offered.

I told him that, over and above anything else I might do, I would undertake to run Macy's business conferences in a way that would make them so effective that it would reduce their frequency as well as the time the top executives of the company had to spend away from their desks and the important work they did in their private offices, to assemble for hours around a conference table in a meeting room.

When Macy's Chairman quickly calculated the annual salaries of his top executives and figured out the saving and efficiency that might result from less time spent in business conferences, accompanied by better results attained through them, he did not hesitate for a moment to say that, if I could do what I promised, I would more than earn my salary. (I did not take the job for reasons of no relevance here.)

Everything I have said about business conferences applies with equal force to faculty meetings in our colleges and universities, to the meetings of physicians on a hospital staff to decide matters of policy, and to the sessions at which the directors of foundations and other nonprofit corporations come together to solve their practical problems and reach decisions affecting their future actions.

· 4 ·

The public discussion of public issues, by the people at large as well as by those in public office or the candidates for such offices, is the lifeblood of the republic.

A republic in which there is no discussion of the res publica—the public things that we refer to as public affairs—is as much a caricature of its true self as would be a military organization in which there is no armament and no consideration of the strategy and tactics for the use of arms.

It makes no difference whether the republic involves direct participation of all its citizens or is a representative form of government in which both the people as a whole and elected or selected officials participate. The agoras and forums of the republics of antiquity in Greece and Rome testify to the role that public discussion played in their lives.

SPQR (*Senatus Populusque Romanus* — the Senate and

People of Rome), that symbol of the Roman Republic while it prospered, signified participation by both the patricians and the plebs, the senators and the people, in government. This always involved them in the public discussion of public issues.

When the imperial and despotic rule of the Caesars displaced republican government, discussion ceased. The people came together only in the amphitheatre or at the circus to indulge in more or less brutal pastimes, but certainly not to discuss public issues. The senators took to their homes and tried to avoid any suspicion that they might have something to say about public affairs. The republic died when discussion ceased and the Caesars, with their pretorian guards, took over the reins of government.

Modern republics, most of them in the form of representative government, have their parliaments, congresses, diets, or otherwise named legislative assemblies, in the place of the agoras and forums of the ancient republics. The word "parliament" is the most significant of these various names because its etymology signifies that this branch of government involves speech or talk, the kind of speech or talk, of course, that is concerned with res publica.

The amendments to the constitution of our own republic, which call for the right of the people to assemble and for the protection of freedom of speech, are still another indication of the importance of unfettered public discussion for the life of a republic.

The enforcement of these constitutional provisions may guarantee that public discussion of public issues goes on unfettered, but it does not and cannot ensure that the discussion is as good as it should be, either by the people's representatives in Congress or by the people themselves when they assemble for the purpose of political discussion.

This cannot be secured by any constitutional enactment or any act of government. Improvement in the quality of public discussion and political debate can be achieved only by improvement in the quality of the schooling that the people as a whole receive.

That improvement must, above all, include improvement in their ability to speak and listen well enough to engage effectively in two-way talk, as well as an enlargement of their understanding of the basic political ideas and principles that underlie the framework of our government.

Before the era of universal suffrage and the coming into existence of a democratic republic, it may have been proper to confine such schooling to the few who were then citizens. But now that "we, the people" means "we, the whole adult and sane population," requisite schooling of improved quality must be given to all and be the same for all. It must be as universal as universal suffrage.

The introductory volume that Robert Hutchins wrote for *Great Books of the Western World*, when that set of books was published many years ago by Encyclopaedia Britannica, Inc., carried the title *The Great Conversation*. It refers to that long and continuing conversation about common themes among the writers of the great books that constitutes the tradition of Western thought, or at least its basic framework.

In producing the *Syntopicon*, which also accompanied the set, I attempted to document Robert Hutchins's conception of the great conversation by assembling under almost 3,000 topics of conversation, references to passages in the great books in which this or that topic was discussed by all or almost all of the authors.

In the opening paragraph of *The Great Conversation*, Hutchins not only declared that the Western tradition is most strikingly embodied in the great conversation, but he also pointed out that the defining characteristic of Western civilization lies in the fact that it, and it alone, is the civilization of the dialogue. I cannot refrain from quoting that whole paragraph.

The tradition of the West is embodied in the Great Conversation that began in the dawn of history and that continues to the present day. Whatever the merits of other civilizations in other respects, no civilization is like that of the West in this respect. No other civilization can claim that its defining characteristic is a dialogue of this sort. No dialogue in any other civilization can compare with that of the West in the number of great works of the mind that have contributed to this dialogue. The goal toward which Western society moves is the Civilization of the Dialogue. The spirit of Western civilization is the spirit of inquiry. Its dominant element is the *Logos*. Nothing is to remain undiscussed. Everybody is to speak his mind. No proposition is to be left unexamined. The exchange of ideas is held to be the path to the realization of the potentialities of the race.

The writing of dialogues for the purpose of exhibiting philosophical thought, which is nothing but thought about the most fundamental ideas, begins with the Greeks, continues with the Romans, takes a somewhat different form in the oral disputations at mediaeval universities, which Thomas Aquinas, for example, records at length in written form, and persists into modern times with dialogues written by Bishop Berkeley, David Hume, and others.

In his essay on *Civil Liberty*, Hume acknowledges the centrality of conversation in human life and society, and praises the French for improving on the Greeks in this respect.

In one respect the French have excelled even the Greeks. They have perfected the art, the most useful and agreeable of any, *l'art de vivre*, the art of society and conversation.

With all due respect to the French, conversation flourished in eighteenth-century England and at the same time in the American colonies. Without it, this republic might never have come into existence. Conversation began to dwindle and wither away only toward the end of the nineteenth century, a tendency that has reached its nadir in our time. That decline runs parallel to the decline in the quality of public education as the population of our schools increased from the few to the many and from the many to all the children who would become the future citizens of our land.

· 5 ·

Finally, let us go from national and local politics to the international scene. There the importance of conversation reaches its maximum. International wars begin when diplomatic conversations between nations fail. They are presaged by newspaper reports to the effect that "conversations are deteriorating" or that they have "broken down." Then, if the conflict of interests between nations is sufficiently serious, there is nothing left for them to do but fight to secure their national interests.

This point was made most eloquently by Cicero in the first century of our era. He wrote:

There are two ways of settling disputed questions; one by discussion, the other by force. The first being characteristic of men, the second of brutes, we should have recourse to the latter only if the former fails.

The same fundamental insight was expressed centuries later in somewhat different words by the Italian, Machiavelli, and by the Englishman, John Locke. Machiavelli wrote:

. . . there are two methods of fighting, the one by law, the other by force: the first method is that of men, the second of beasts; but as the first method is often insufficient, one must have recourse to the second.

Locke's statement of the same point comes to us as follows:

There are two sorts of contests among men, the one managed by law, the other by force; and these are of such a nature that where the one ends, the other always begins.

Fighting by law or managing tc settle contests by law, in Machiavelli's and Locke's phrasing of the matter, amount to the same thing that Cicero had in mind when he wrote that the first way of settling disputes is by discussion, not force. The legal adjudication of any dispute or conflict of interests always involves discussion. If the decision reached is legally enforced, such force represents that monopoly of authorized force possessed only by a duly constituted government. All other force, unauthorized, is violence. The use of it is criminal violence, terrorism, or war.

War is nothing but the field of force. What we call the "cold war" does not consist in the use of force or the resort to violent measures. Even if actual warfare has not yet begun, it is truly a state of war, not peace, because it is a situation in which conflicts or disputes cannot be completely settled by discussion or by legal decisions that are enforceable by authorized force.

Peace, then, genuine civil peace, not the cold war, which is nothing but the absence of actual warfare, exists wherever the apparatus is available for settling all disputes or conflicts by discussion and by resort to law and its enforcement.

Civil government provides the apparatus needed for maintaining conversation or discussion as a way of settling disputes. When the machinery of government operates as it should, it does not allow conversation to deteriorate to the point where individuals or nations must resort to the use of force—the method of brutes in the jungle, not the method of humans in civilized society.

The lesson to be learned from this understanding of war and peace is that world civil peace requires enforceable world civil government, exactly as every unit of local civil peace requires enforceable local civil government.

I am fully aware that this lesson will come as a hopeless fantasy or as a counsel of despair to most people. Their immediate reaction will be to say that world civil government, federal in structure akin to the national government of the United States, is an unrealizable utopian dream. If they are inveterate in their parochial nationalism, they are likely to go further and dismiss it as undesirable because it calls for a surrender of national sovereignty.

My response to such reactions is that world government is not only desirable for the sake of world peace, without which the human race may not survive on this planet, it is also both necessary and possible. It is just as possible as the formation of the federal republic of the United States by the surrender of sovereignty by the thirteen American colonies after they had won their independence and after they found themselves at serious odds with one another during the period they loosely coexisted under the Articles of Confederation, which united them as loosely as the United Nations are united.

In the first nine *Federalist Papers* written by Hamilton, Madison, and Jay in favor of adopting the Constitution of the United States to replace the Articles of Confederation, the argument advanced for federal union—a more perfect union, as the Preamble to the Constitution declares—goes right to the point.

The writers argue that, under the Articles of Confederation, the several now independent states in the new world are likely to go to war with one another, for the same reason that the nations of the old world are perpetually at war with one another. If they were alive today, they would argue similarly that the Charter of the United Nations is no better an instrument for preventing war than the Articles of Confederation.

I need add only one thing more. In 1946, after the dropping of the first atomic bombs, which grew out of the nuclear fission first produced at the University of Chicago, Robert Hutchins, then its President, created a Committee to Frame a Constitution for World Government. After two years of thought and discussion, the Committee produced a document that was published by the University of Chicago under the title *Preliminary Draft of a World Constitution*.

That document, in my opinion, provides grounds for thinking that world government is not only necessary for world peace, but also quite possible. The only matter left in doubt is the probability of its coming into existence before it is too late to prevent a war that can destroy this planet or preclude the survival of civilized life upon it.

pronship and pleasurable conversation with others about
the discoveries of travel, about books read, about know-

· 6 ·

In conclusion, let me call attention to the role that conversation plays in the private life of every individual who
has ample free time to be spent in the pursuits of leisure—
not the activities of play that result in recreation or relaxation, but activities that contribute to learning and to the
mental, moral, and spiritual growth of the individual.

The pursuits of leisure may be activities in which individuals engage in a completely solitary fashion, such as
reading and writing, or artistic productions of any kind
wherein individuals work by themselves. Or they may be
social activities in which individuals engage with one another, such as conversation or two-way talk. When intellectual work of any kind, artistic or scientific and scholarly,
is undertaken cooperatively by a number of persons associated in the enterprise, it will also involve conversation or
discussion.

Engagement in the pursuits of leisure in the mature years
of one's life is absolutely indispensable to completing the
educational process which schooling barely begins but for
which it should prepare. Without continued learning
throughout all the years of one's adult life, no one can
become a truly educated person, no matter how good the
individual's schooling has been.

What are the major and most universal forms that such
continued learning should take? My answer is threefold.

One form of learning consists in the discoveries about
life and society that individuals make in the course of their
experience. A second consists in the increasing knowledge
and enlarged understanding derived from the reading of
books that can provide such goods. The third consists in
the benefits conferred upon the individual by engaging in

profitable and pleasurable conversation with others about the discoveries of travel, about books read, about knowledge acquired, and about things understood.

The first two without the third fall short of the consummation to be sought for the process of continued learning in adult life. To consummate that process is to become an educated human being. That is why learning how to speak and listen well are of such great importance to us all.

Appendices

Appendices

THE HARVEY CUSHING MEMORIAL ORATION,
delivered at the annual meeting of the American Association of Neurological Surgeons, April 1982

INTRODUCTION

1. I am greatly honored by your invitation to deliver the Harvey Cushing Memorial Address—or Oration, as it is referred to. An address I hope it will be; but an oration, I think not.

2. More than honored, I am somewhat overawed, coming as I do from the soft science of psychology and the even softer discipline known as philosophy, and standing before you who are leading representatives of a science that is hard down to its core.

   a. When Dr. Kemp Clark first approached me, I was hesitant to accept. I do not know whether it was the eloquence expected of an orator that frightened me, or the eminence of Harvey Cushing that made me hesitant.

   b. What overcame my scruples on these two counts were the many memories that soon crowded into my mind—not only the recollection of my great admiration for Dr. Cushing, but also the memory of how far back in my life and how deep in my intellectual interest lay the study of neurophysiology.

   c. In an early telephone conversation with Dr. Clark, I told him that while a young instructor in psychology at Columbia University in the early 1920s I went down to the College of Physicians and Surgeons, then located at 59th Street near 10th Avenue, to take a course in neuroanatomy with Professors Tilney and Elwyn.

(1) Professor Elwyn was the anatomist who gave us most of the lectures and supervised our microscopic examination of slides of spinal sections.

(2) Dr. Tilney was one of the great neurologists of his day. I remember vividly his coming in a dinner suit to an evening lecture to tell us about his diagnosis of brain pathology and about the surgical procedures involved in its therapy.

3. As a student and teacher of psychology, I could not help but be interested in the workings of the brain and central nervous system.

a. The early chapters of William James's two volume *Principles of Psychology* were filled with speculations about the relation of mind and brain, as were Ladd and Woodworth's *Elements of Physiological Psychology*. Both books, if you were to read them today, would greatly amuse you by the extent of the ignorance that then passed for scientific knowledge.

b. In more recent years, my reading in this field has included many books of much more recent vintage. Let me just mention a few in passing.

C. S. Sherrington's *Integrative Action of the Nervous System*

C. Judson Herrick's *The Brains of Rats and Men*

J. C. Eccles's *The Neurophysiological Basis of Mind*

Ward Halstead's *Brain and Intelligence*

Warren McCulloch's *Embodiments of Mind*

K. S. Lashley's *Brain Mechanisms and Intelligence*

Wilder Penfield's essay "The Physiological Basis of the Mind," in *Control of the Mind*

c.   Even more recently, the rise of experimental researches and technological advances in the field of artificial intelligence has opened up another vein of interest in the physical basis of mind, and I have turned to such books as:

John von Neumann's *The Computer and the Brain*

Minds and Machines, a collection of papers edited by A. R. Anderson

A. M. Turning's essay "Computing Machinery and Intelligence"

J. Z. Young's *Programs of the Brain*

Daniel C. Dennett's very recent *Brainstorms*

d.   Please forgive me for what may appear to be pretension to some erudition in a field in which you are all experts. I mention my excursions into the literature of neurophysiology and of artificial intelligence in order to allay the suspicion that may arise in your minds when I proceed now to deal philosophically—even metaphysically— with the problem of the relation of mind to brain.

(1)   You might suspect that my philosophical speculations reflect ancient and

venerable theories that no longer stand up in the light of the facts uncovered by the most advanced scientific research.

(2)   You might even suspect that since I am going to talk to you as a philosopher, I might feel justified in doing so in cavalier ignorance of relevant scientific knowledge bearing on the matters to be considered.

(3)   I would like to assure you that neither suspicion is justified. I may not be as well-informed with regard to the most recent advances in neurophysiology as I should be, but I hope you will find that my philosophical consideration of mind and brain does not fly in the face of facts that must be taken into account.

4. The two main questions that I would like to consider with you can be stated as follows.

   a.   Will our knowledge of the brain and nervous system, both central and autonomic, either now or in the future, suffice to explain all aspects of animal behavior?

   b.   On the supposition that the answer to that question is affirmative, then the second question is: Does this mean that we will also succeed in explaining human behavior, especially human thought, in terms of what we know, now or in the future, about the human brain and nervous system?

c. You will observe at once, I am sure, that the answer to the second question, in the light of an affirmative answer to the first question, depends on one crucial point: whether the difference between human beings and brute animals is a difference in kind or in degree.

5. To probe and ponder the answers to these two questions, I propose to proceed as follows.

a. First, briefly to explain the distinction between difference in kind and difference in degree, and especially the two modes of difference in kind—radical and superficial.

b. Second, to illustrate a radical difference in kind by considering humans in relation to angels and to eliminate what I hope you will agree is an erroneous view of the relation of mind to brain.

c. Third, to consider humans in relation to brutes and also in relation to machines devised to embody artificial intelligence.

d. And, finally, to propose what I hold to be the correct view of the relation of the human mind to the human brain—correct, that is, until future experimental research in neurophysiology and in the sphere of artificial intelligence succeeds in refuting it.

DIFFERENCES IN KIND AND IN DEGREE

1. A difference in degree exists between two things when one is more and the other is less in a given specified respect.

   a. Thus, for example, two lines of unequal length differ only in degree.

   b. Similarly, two brains of unequal weight or complexity differ only in degree.

2. A difference in kind exists between two things when one possesses a property or attribute that the other totally lacks.

   a. Thus, for example, a rectangle and a circle differ in kind for one has interior angles and the other totally lacks them.

   b. So, too, a vertebrate organism that has a brain and central nervous system differs in kind from organisms that totally lack these organs.

3. A difference in kind is superficial if it is based upon and can be explained by an underlying difference in degree.

   a. Thus for example, the apparent difference in kind between water and ice (you can walk on one and not the other) can be explained by the rate of motion of their component molecules, which is an underlying difference in degree.

   b. Similarly, the apparent difference in kind between humans and other animals (things that human beings can do that other animals cannot do at all) may be explainable in terms of the degree of complexity of their brains. If that is so, then the apparent difference in kind is superficial.

4. A difference in kind is radical if it cannot be explained in terms of any underlying difference in degree, but only by the presence of a factor in one that is totally absent in the other.

   a. Consider the difference between plants and the higher animals. This appears to be a difference in kind, for the animals perform operations totally absent in plants.

   b. If this difference in kind can be explained only in terms of the presence in animals and the absence in plants of brains and nervous systems, then it is a radical, not a superficial, difference in kind.

ANGELS AND HUMAN BEINGS

1. Let me begin by saying that I wish you to consider angels only as possible beings—as purely hypothetical entities. Whether or not there is any truth in the religious belief that angels really exist need not concern us.

   a. As possible beings, angels are purely spiritual. Our interest in them here arises from the fact that they are conceived as minds *without* bodies.

      (1) As minds without bodies, angels know and will and love, but not in the same manner that we do.

(2)   Their lack of bodies has a number of striking consequences.

    (a)   They do not learn from experience.

    (b)   They do not think discursively for they have no imaginations and memories.

    (c)   Their knowledge, which is intuitive, derives from innate ideas implanted in them at the moment of their creation.

    (d)   They speak to one another telepathically without the use of any medium of communication.

    (e)   Their minds, which are infallible, never go to sleep.

b.   In all these respects, minds without bodies differ from the human mind precisely because the latter is associated with a body and depends upon that body for *some* or *all* of its functions.

2.   You may question the possibility of angels—of minds without bodies, minds without brains. If so, let me defend the possibility of angels against the materialists who think they have grounds for denying that angels are possible. I do so because, as you will see presently, the error of the materialists has a critical bear-

ing on the course of my treatment of the problem of minds and brains.

    a.   The argument of the materialists runs as follows.

        (1)   They assert that nothing exists in reality except corporeal things, from elementary particles up to the most complex organisms, from atoms to stars and galaxies.

        (2)   But angels are said to be incorporeal.

        (3)   Therefore, they conclude, angels are impossible, as inconceivable and impossible as are round squares.

    b.   The argument is weak in one respect and faulty in another.

        (1)   Its initial premise (that nothing except corporeal things exist) is an unproved and unprovable assumption. It may be true, but we have no grounds for asserting its truth, neither with certitude nor even beyond a reasonable doubt. It is as much a matter of faith as the religious belief in the reality of angels.

        (2)   Even if we were to grant the truth of that initial premise, the argument is faulty, because the conclusion does not follow.

(a)   If the premise assumed were true, the valid conclusion to be drawn from it is that angels—incorporeal beings—*do not* exist in reality.

(b)   But the conclusion that angels *cannot* exist—that they are impossible—does not follow at all.

c.   There are many positive arguments to support the conceivability and possibility of angels, but I am not going to take the time to set them before you. For our present purposes, let it suffice for us to recognize that the exponents of materialism cannot validly deny the possibility of angels.

d.   This being so, neither can they deny that the human mind may be a spiritual—an immaterial factor—associated with the brain as a corporeal factor, both of which are needed to explain human thought.

3. This brings us to a view at the opposite extreme from materialism, a view that looks upon the human mind as an immaterial substance, an immaterial power, that does not need a brain for its unique activity, which is rational thought.

a.   This is the view taken by Plato in antiquity and by Descartes at the beginning of modern times.

b. It commits what I have called an angelistic fallacy, for it regards the rational soul or human intellect as if it were an incarnate angel—a mind that, in humans, may be associated with a body, but one that does not depend upon or need a body for its intellectual operations.

c. I do not have to persuade you, in the light of all you know about the dependence of human mental operations upon brain functions and processes, and all you know about the effects of brain pathology upon human thought, that this Platonic and Cartesian view of the human mind as an incarnate angel flies in the face of well attested evidence, and must therefore be rejected.

d. I wish only to add that, on purely philosophical grounds, the dualism of mind or soul and body does not stand up.

   (1) It denies the unity of the human being. It makes us a duality of two independent substances—as independent as a boat and person who is rowing it. Either one of the two can cease to exist without the other ceasing to exist. They are existentially distinct and separable, as our mind and our brain are not.

   (2) It leaves us with an inexplicable mystery of why the human mind should have any association with a human body.

HUMAN BEINGS, OTHER ANIMALS—AND INTELLIGENT MACHINES

1. There is no question that in many behavioral respects we differ from other animals only in degree.

2. Nor is there any question that the human brain differs from the brains of the higher mammals in degree—in complexity and in the ratio of brain weight to body weight.

3. There may be some question as to whether human and animal brains also differ in kind. I would like to leave this question for you to answer.

    a. For example, is the asymmetry of the human brain's left and right lobes uniquely human?

    b. Is the absence in animal brains of anything like the motor center for speech, which seems to be connected with cortical asymmetry, a difference in kind?

    c. Is the special character of the very large frontal lobe of the human brain another indication of a neurological difference in kind?

4. Whatever answers you give to these questions should be considered in the light of what I am now going to say about behavioral differences in kind between humans and brutes.

    a. Here are the differences between humans and brutes that I think are differences in kind, not in degree. Whether these differences in kind are superficial or radical remains to be seen.

(1)   Animals are capable only of perceptual thought, whereas humans are capable of conceptual thought, which is totally absent in animals.

(a)   Conceptual and syntactical speech, with a vocabulary of words that refer to imperceptible and unimaginable objects, together with the way in which humans learn speech, is one indication of this. It is unrefuted by all the recent work on so-called speech by chimpanzees and bottle-nosed dolphins.

(b)   Animal perceptual thought, involving perceptual abstractions and generalizations, cannot deal with any object that is not perceptible or that is not perceptually present.

(c)   Human conceptual thought, in sharp contrast, deals with objects that are not perceptually present and with objects that are totally imperceptible—with angels, for example.

(2) This basic difference between perceptual and conceptual thought, and the fact that man uniquely possesses the power of conceptual thought, explains many other differences between human and animal behavior.

(a) Man is the only animal with an extended historical tradition and with cultural, as opposed to merely genetic, continuity between the generations.

(b) Man is the only animal that makes laws and constitutions for the associations he forms

(c) Man is the only animal that makes machinery and that produces things by machinofacturing.

(d) None of these things, and others like them, would be possible without conceptual thought and conceptual speech.

5. If I am right concerning the existence of behavioral differences in kind between humans and brutes, we must face the question that still remains: Is this difference in kind superficial or radical? Can it be explained in terms of differences in degree between humans and animals? If so, it is only superficial. If not, it is radical.

a. One other condition must be satisfied in order for us to conclude that the difference is only superficial. The difference in degree between human and animal brains must itself provide us with an adequate explanation of the apparent difference in kind between human and animal behavior.

b. Let me table that question for a moment in order, first, to consider the human mind in relation to the machines that are supposed to embody artificial intelligence—intelligence that differs only in degree from human intelligence.

c. I do this because it will have a critical bearing on the ultimate question to be resolved.

6. Here the most important thing to point out is that the difference between the human brain and the artifacts supposedly endowed by their makers with intelligence lies in the fact that the latter are purely electrical networks, whereas the human brain is a chemical factory as well as an electrical network, and the chemistry of the brain is indispensable to its electrical operation.

a. The extraordinary researches of the last thirty years have shown us how important the chemical facilitators and transmitters are to the operations of the human brain.

b. These are absent from the functioning of artificial intelligence machines so far, though there is now some movement in the direction of creating what are called "wet computers."

c.   Until that is fully realized, there will remain a
     difference in kind between the human brain and
     computers, one that would not be removed even
     if machines could be constructed that had elec-
     trical units and connections in excess of ten raised
     to the eleventh power.

d.   If the dream of wet computers is not fully real-
     ized, neurophysiology may some day be able to
     explain human thought, but we will never be
     able to construct a machine, no matter how
     complex and refined electrically, that will think
     the way that human beings do.

e.   We can train dogs and horses to do very compli-
     cated and remarkable tricks that have nothing to
     do with their possessing intelligence of an ex-
     traordinary or remarkable sort.

f.   So, too, we can program computers to do even
     more complicated and more extraordinary tricks
     that are amazing counterfeits of human thought,
     but this does not mean that they have the power
     of human thought.

g.   If the only difference between men and brutes
     was the relative size and complexity of the ner-
     vous machinery, aided and abetted by the prod-
     ucts of brain chemistry, then wet computers
     might be constructed to think as well as men.
     They might do better if future computers ex-
     ceed the human brain's componentry by some
     power greater than ten raised to the eleventh
     power and if something analogous to all the hu-

man brain's chemical agents are operative in a so-called wet computer.

h.   However, if the difference between men and brutes is not purely a quantitative difference in brain weight and complexity, relative to body size and weight;

if, instead, the difference between the perceptual power of brutes and the conceptual power of humans stems from the presence in man of an immaterial factor—the human intellect that co-operates with the brain but whose operations are not reducible to brain processes;

then no computer, regardless of how extensive its componentry and how chemically assisted is its electrical circuitry, will ever be able to think, or to engage in conceptual thought as human beings do.

i.   As Descartes said centuries ago, *matter cannot think*. The best computer that ever can be made by man will always be, electrically and chemically, nothing but a material thing.

j.   That is why the test proposed by A. M. Turing of whether computers will ever be able to think in human fashion is so interesting and so significant.

k.   It is an answer to Descartes's challenge to the materialists of his day, defying them to build a machine that could think intellectually.

7. The Turing game is the only critical test that I know whereby to determine whether computers can think in the way in which human beings think. A. M. Turing, by the way, was the somewhat mad English genius who broke the German enigma code.

    a.   The Turing test is based on the following game as a model.

        (1)   An interrogator stands in front of a screen behind which are a male and female human being.

        (2)   The interrogator, by asking them questions and considering the answers they give in written form, must try to determine which one of the persons is a male and which a female.

        (3)   The persons behind the screen must do their intelligent best to deceive the interrogator. If they do their intelligent best, they will succeed.

        (4)   The interrogator's determination will be no better than a guess on his part—fifty percent right, fifty percent wrong.

    b.   Now, says Turing, place a human being and a computer behind the screen, and let the computer have what Turing calls infant or initial programming.

    c.   To understand the limitations of machine-programming, no matter how elaborate and extensive it can become, it is necessary to distinguish between two kinds of innate endowment possessed by the higher mammals and human beings. In contrast to the higher mammals and human beings, the instinctively determined performances of insects are like the kind of innate endowment that consists in the infant programming of machines.

d. Let us consider, first, human beings and the higher mammals. Both have two kinds of innate endowment.

    (1) The first kind is what might be called "programming," borrowing that word from computer technology.

        (a) Programming consists in an animal's innate endowment with determinate preformed responses to stimuli.

        (b) Insects with very elaborate patterns of instinctive behavior have such innate endowment to a very high degree.

        (c) The higher mammals have fewer such preformed patterns of instinctive behavior than the insects do.

        (d) Human beings have the fewest of all: they have no instincts, in the strict sense of that term. Their innate programming consists solely in a relatively small number of spinal and cerebrospinal reflexes.

(2)   The second kind of native endowment consists in abilities or powers that are indeterminate in the sense that they are subject to determination by learning and by the formation of habits. At birth and prior to any determination by learning and habit formation, innate abilities are indeterminate; that is, they do not tend to produce one rather than another type of actual behavior.

(a)   The higher mammals are innately endowed with such abilities and are capable of learning and habit formation, as the training of domestic animals so plainly manifests.

(b)   Human beings have such innate endowment to the highest degree: they are preeminently learning animals whose conduct after birth is largely the result of the determinate development of their innate abilities by learning and habit formation.

(c)   Thus, for example, the human infant is endowed with the ability to learn any language, and has no determinate tendency to speak one rather than another. The human is also endowed with the innate ability to think anything that is thinkable.

e.   Let us next consider humans and machines. In contrast to human beings and the higher mammals, artificial intelligence machines have *only one kind of native endowment*, the kind that Turing calls infant or initial programming.

(1)   Such programming produces always and only determinate preformed behavior on the part of the machine. The machine's programmed performances are exactly like the elaborate instinctive performances of insects or like reflexes in the higher mammals and in man.

(2)   As Hubert L. Dreyfuss points out in his book *What Computers Can't Do*, the kind of innate endowment involved in the programming of machines produces prescribed, determinate perfor-

mances on the part of the machine, never indeterminate abilities, rendered determinate by learning and habit formation.

(a)   In the case of animals, such learning and habit formation takes place by conditioning.

(b)   In the case of humans, it takes place by conditioning in some instances and by free choice in others.

(3)   To quote Professor Dreyfuss, "nonprogrammable human capacities are involved in all forms of intelligent behavior," and it is precisely such nonprogrammable abilities that cannot be put into machines.

f.   This being the case, the initial or infant programming of an artificial intelligence machine will never be able to succeed in the Turing test.

(1)   No matter how great such programming is in the endowment of the machine with preformed responses to N questions (where N is any finite number however large), there will always be the N-plus-1 question to which the machine will have no preformed response, and so the interrogator will be able to detect the machine behind the screen, because the human behind the

screen will be able to answer the N-plus-1 question.

(2) Of course, it remains possible that machines can someday be given the second kind of innate development—indeterminate abilities subject to determination by learning, by habit formation, by conditioning, or by choice.

(3) I think—and so does Professor Dreyfuss—that this is highly unlikely. But the only way that we can empirically discover that it borders on the impossible is to have the artificial intelligence experts try and try again and fail each time. The more times they try and the more times they fail, the greater the probability that they cannot succeed.

8. If it turns out to be impossible for machines to perform in a way that is indistinguishable from human performance, as I think it will, then we will be justified on an empirical basis in concluding that man's distinctive performance is not explicable solely in terms of the electrochemical power of his brain.

a. If it were, then future machines, which can be given more electrochemical power than that possessed by the human brain, would certainly be able to outperform man and outperform man in a manner that is indistinguishable from human performance.

b.   The conclusion we have reached confirms Aristotle's and Aquinas's philosophical judgment that the brain is *only a necessary and not the sufficient condition* for human thought. We cannot think without our brains, but we do not think with them. We think with an essentially immaterial power—the power of the human intellect.

c.   If I turn out to be wrong about this—and only the future will tell—then I am prepared to concede that machines can think the way human beings do, and that physical processes, whether merely electrical or electrochemical, can provide us with an adequate explanation of human conceptual thought as well as of animal perceptual thought.

9. Before I go on, let me call your attention to three matters that are connected with or emerge from our consideration of the Turing test.

a.   The first is the historic fact that the seventeenth-century philosopher, Descartes, anticipated Turing by proposing a similar test to show that machines—and animals, which he regarded as machines with senses and brains but without intellects—cannot think. It was a conversational test. No machine will ever be built, Descartes said, that will be able to engage in conversation in the way in which two human beings engage in conversation that is infinitely flexible and unpredictable in the turns that it will take.

b.   Whether or not the Turing machine, contrary to Descartes's prediction, will ever be built, it is certainly clear that no talking chimpanzee or dolphin, using its sign language, could ever pass the Turing test of being indistinguishable from a human being behind the screen.

c. Whether or not you think that the difference in kind between humans and brutes is superficial or radical depends on whether you think some day that neurophysiology will some day be able to explain how human beings can succeed in the Turing test.

    (1) Is so, will the power of the human brain account for such success?

    (2) Or will some other factor—some immaterial factor, such as Descartes thought the human intellect to be—be needed to explain it?

MINDS AND BRAINS

1. We have already encountered two extreme views of the relation of the human mind or intellect to the human brain.

a. At one extreme, there is the materialist who denies not only the reality, but also the possibility of immaterial beings, powers, or operations.

    (1) On this materialist view, brain action and processes provide the necessary and also the sufficient conditions for all mental operations, human conceptual thought as well as animal perceptual thought.

(2)   This view has come to be called the identity hypothesis. The word "identity" signifies that mind and brain are existentially inseparable. The word "hypothesis" concedes that it is an unproved—and, I think, also unprovable—assumption.

(3)   The identity hypothesis takes two forms, one more extreme than the other.

    (a)   The more extreme form is known as "reductive materialism." It claims that there is not even an analytical distinction between the action of the mind and the action of the brain.

    (b)   The less extreme form—in my judgment much more in accord with the indisputable facts—admits that any description of brain processes is always analytically distinct from any description of mental processes. This is just as true of animal perceptual thought as it is true of human conceptual thought. Conceding the analytical difference between brain processes and thought processes, this less extreme form of materialism nevertheless insists that mind and brain are existentially inseparable, and so brain action should be able to explain all acts of the mind, both conceptual and perceptual.

(4) On this hypothesis, tenable in its less extreme form, neurophysiology should be able to succeed in explaining all aspects of human intelligence as well as all aspects of animal intelligence. The furthest reaches of human thought should not escape its explanatory powers.

b. At the other extreme, there are the immaterialists who deny that brain processes can now, or will ever be able to, explain human thought.

(1) On this view, brain action is neither a necessary, nor a sufficient condition for thought.

(2) This immaterialist view takes its most extreme form in the philosophy of Bishop Berkeley, who denied the very existence of matter, and, therefore, regarded humans as purely spiritual creatures, no less spirits than the angels in heaven.

(3)   The extreme form of immaterialism flies in the face of indisputable facts, just as the extreme form of materialism does. We should, therefore, have no hesitation in rejecting both of these extremes.

(4)   The less extreme form of immaterialism is, as we have already observed, the Platonic and Cartesian view of the rational soul or the human intellect as an incarnate angel, somehow incarcerated in a human body—a purely spiritual substance dwelling in a body that it in no way needs for its essential operation, which is rational thought.

(5)   Just one fact—and one negative fact is always quite sufficient—casts grave doubt on the Platonic and Cartesian view. Angels, as I pointed out, never sleep. Their intellects are always active. Human beings do fall asleep and wake up. Their intellects are sometimes inactive. We may dream from time to time, but we are not always thinking. That fact is inexplicable on the Cartesian and Platonic view of the intellect's relation to the human body and brain.

2. In between these two extreme views, each in its several forms, lies the only view that recommends itself to me as fitting all the facts we know. It fits everything we know about the nature of human thought

and about the limitations of matter and its physical properties.

a. This middle view is a moderate materialism combined with an equally moderate immaterialism.

b. Its moderate materialism consists in its accepting two tenets held by the less extreme form of the identity hypothesis.

(1) The first of these tenets is that brain processes and mental processes are analytically distinguishable. No description of the one can ever be substituted for a description of the other.

(2) This view also agrees that brain processes are at least a necessary condition for the occurrence of mental processes—something that is denied by the extreme forms of immaterialism.

c. The middle view that I espouse is also materialistic to the extent that it concedes that every aspect of perceptual thought, in humans as well as in other animals—all the acts of sense perception, imagination, and memory, as well as emotions, passions, and desires—can be or will someday be explained entirely in neurophysiological terms. There is nothing immaterial or spiritual about any of the behavioral or mental operations that are common to human beings and other animals.

d. What is immaterialistic about this middle view— and quite moderately immaterialistic—can be summed up by saying that human thought (that is, distinctively conceptual thought) cannot now, and never will, be explained in terms of brain action. Nor can the freedom of the human will—the freedom of choice that is distinctively human—ever be explained in terms of physical causation or the motions of material particles.

(1)   In other words, without the acts of perception, imagination, and memory, all of which are acts of the sense organs and the brain, conceptual thought cannot occur.

(2)   Mental pathology and disabilities, aphasias of all sorts, senile dementia, and so on, indicate plainly the role of the brain in the life of the mind. But that is a limited role.

e.   Perhaps the most precise way of summarizing this middle view is as follows.

(1)   We see with our eyes and with the visual cortex of the brain. We hear with our ears and with the acoustical cortex of the brain.

(2)   But what organ do we think with? What is the organ of conceptual thought? The middle view answers: *not with the brain*. We do not think conceptually with our brains, even if we cannot think conceptually without our brains.

(3) In short, the brain is a necessary, but not the sufficient, condition of conceptual thought. On this one crucial point, the middle view differs from the less extreme form of the immaterialist or the nonidentity hypothesis—the view of Plato and Descartes.

(4) This means that an immaterial factor or power—the human intellect and will—is involved in cooperation with the human body in the production of conceptual thought and free choice.

(5) And this, if true, as I think it is, means that the difference in kind between human beings and other animals, not to mention machines, is a radical, not a superficial, difference in kind.

(6) It also means that mankind occupies a position on the boundary line between the whole realm of corporeal creatures and the realm of spiritual beings, the angels and God, whether these be regarded as mere possibilities or are believed in as actual.

(7) But mankind, in this middle position, does not straddle the line that divides the material from the spiritual, with one foot in each realm, as Plato and Descartes would have us think. Mankind is mainly in the realm of corporeal things, but by the power of his

immaterial intellect, he is able to reach
over into the spiritual realm.

CONCLUDING REFLECTIONS

1. Permit me a few concluding reflections. I am relatively certain of only two things.

   a.   One is that failure to concede the indispensable
        role of the brain in human thought is an angelis-
        tic fallacy that must be rejected.

   b.   The other is that the materialistic denial of the
        possibility of spiritual substances and of imma-
        terial powers, such as the human intellect, must
        also be rejected.

2. With somewhat less assurance, I am persuaded by
everything I know that brain action by itself does not
and cannot suffice to explain conceptual thought, because the essential character of such thought involves
transcendence of all material conditions. The reach of
the human mind to objects of thought that are totally
imperceptible and totally unimaginable is the clearest
indication of this.

3. Where does this leave us? As I see it, with these two
conclusions:

   a.   All aspects of animal behavior, animal intelli-
        gence, and animal mentality—all below the level
        of conceptual thought—can be or will someday
        be satisfactorily explained by our knowledge of
        the brain and nervous system.

   b.   Such knowledge can now contribute—and in the
        future it will do even more to contribute—to the

explanation of the acts of the human mind, but neurophysiology may never be able to provide a completely satisfactory explanation of conceptual thought and freedom of choice.

NOTE

During the discussion that followed the lecture, questions from the audience led me to summarize the gist of it in two hypothetical propositions.

1. IF humans are superior to brutes *only because* they have larger and more complex brains than brutes, THEN computers will someday be superior to humans.

2. IF humans can do what brutes cannot do at all *only because* of the immateriality of the human intellect, THEN computers will never be able to do the things that so radically differentiate humans from other animals.

There is a metaphysical argument in support of the conditional clause in the second of these hypothetical statements. Since it is not likely to persuade the materialists who affirm the conditional clause in the first of these hypothetical statements, what is at issue here can be put to an empirical test in the following manner.

Let the computer technologists try to build a computer that will be able to perform in conversation in a manner indistinguishable from human performance. Each time that they try and fail, it becomes more and more probable that the metaphysical argument against their success is sound. Should they ever succeed, that would constitute a refutation of the metaphysical argument. The future will tell which is correct.

THE TWELVE DAYS OF THE ASPEN EXECUTIVE
SEMINAR (an address delivered at the Aspen Institute for
Humanistic Studies, August 1972)*

The ultimate objective of the Aspen Executive Seminar is
to enable the participants to come to a better understanding of "democracy" and "capitalism"—the two defining
features of the society in which we live; and also to a better understanding of their opposites—"totalitarianism" and
"communism"; in order thereby to face intelligently and
critically the basic polarizations that confront us in the
world today.

To this end, the readings revolve around four fundamental ideas—the ideas of equality, liberty, justice, and
property—ideas which are indispensable to our understanding of democracy and capitalism, their opposites, and
the issues that result from this opposition.

The aim of the discussions is to get a clearer grasp of
these four ideas, in themselves, in relation to one another,
and in their bearing on such things as the nature of government, the distinction between constitutional and despotic government, the relation of economic to political
democracy, free enterprise, decentralization, and so on.

To achieve this aim, the readings are organized in the
following manner. With few exceptions, the readings for a
given day always include conflicting points of view so that
the participants can be asked to formulate the issues that

---

*This lecture was originally written in the outline form of the Harvey Cush-
ing Oration, reproduced in Appendix I, but, for purposes of publication by the
Aspen Institute, I recast it in ordinary prose paragraphs.

are joined by the writers, and to take sides on those issues, giving reasons for the positions that they take. And in the sequence of twelve sessions, the readings open up in a fan-like fashion, revolving in wider and wider circles about the same four fundamental ideas—comprehending more, enabling the participants progressively to reach deeper and deeper levels of understanding, as each day builds on the days that have preceded it.

What I would like to do in this lecture is, of course, impossible. Using the notes that I have made year after year at the end of each day's discussion, I would like to report to you the actual content of the twelve discussions as they occur in sequence. I make such a report each day to the participants, summarizing the preceding day's discussion. It takes me about twenty minutes to present. Stringing twelve such reports together would take about three hours and a half. I am afraid that is out of the question.

Instead, I am going to try to do the next best thing. I am going to follow through one line of development as it opens up in the course of the twelve sessions. Proceeding in this way, I will not be able to deal in detail with all the readings.* I hope you will bear in mind that what I am presenting tonight is only a taste of the Aspen Readings and of what can be learned from the discussion of them.

One final preliminary and then I am ready to begin. When I speak of what can be learned, I must perforce be reporting what I myself have learned from participation in the Aspen Seminars, as a reader and as a member of the group. I think I dare say, without fear of being too pre-

---

*In most cases, the readings assigned are selections from the books cited for each day, not the whole.

sumptuous, that I have observed other members of the group learning the same things, too, each in his own way.

THE TWELVE DAYS OF THE ASPEN SEMINAR

FIRST MONDAY

An Agreement of the People, 1647

Declaration of Independence, 1776

Benjamin Franklin, *On the Legislative Branch*, 1789

Debate in the New York State Constitutional Convention, 1821

Our era begins not with the Declaration of Independence in 1776, but with the debate that took place more than a hundred years earlier, within the ranks of Cromwell's army, between the Levellers—the exponents of political equality—and the men of property and substance, such as Lord Cromwell himself and his son-in-law, Colonel Ireton.

The question being disputed had never been raised before. It was: Who are *the* people? When we say "We the people," or "Up the People," or "Power to the People," to whom are we referring? The issue, more precisely formulated, was this: Shall there be a substantial property qualification for suffrage, thus restricting the franchise to men of property; or shall all men have a voice in their country's affairs and all be politically equal even though their possession of property or their lack of it makes them economically unequal?

Borrowing terms from Greek political thought and practice, we can say that the issue is a conflict between the oligarchs, who wish to restrict the franchise to the propertied class, and the democrats, who wish to extend it to the unpropertied as well. But though this conflict occurred in the Greek city-states, in antiquity it never went beyond an issue setting the few against the many; whereas the principles enunciated by the Levellers in Cromwell's army raised a question about the rights not of the many, but of all men.

In addition, the Levellers relate political equality to political liberty, introducing for the first time the notion of the consent of the governed. Listen to the words of Sir John Wildman.

Every person in England hath as clear a right to elect his representative as the greatest person in England. I conceive that is the undeniable maxim of government: that all government is in the free consent of the people. If [so], then upon that account there is no person that is under a just government, or hath justly his own, unless he by his own free consent be put under that government. This he cannot be unless he be consenting to it, and therefore, according to this maxim, there is never a person in England [but ought to have a voice in elections]. If [this], as that gentleman says, be true, there are no laws that in this strictness and rigor of justice [any man is bound to], that are not made by those who[m] he doth consent to. And therefore I should humbly move, that if the question be stated—which would soonest bring things to an issue—it might rather be thus: Whether any person can justly be bound by law, who doth not give his consent that such persons shall make laws for him?

What are the arguments on this issue *pro* and *con*? The position of the Levellers, represented by Wildman and Major Rainborough, is as follows.

They appeal to natural rights. Every man has a natural—an inherent human—right to be governed as a free man, that is, with his consent and with his participation in government through an effective suffrage. All should be politically equal even if they are economically unequal, because their equality as human beings, each with an equal right to freedom, entitles them to political equality.

The rejoinder of the oligarchs—Cromwell and Ireton—is as follows. Political liberty belongs only to those who have enough economic independence not to be subservient to the will of others. Only a man of property has such economic independence. Only those who have a fixed and permanent interest in the realm—through their land-holdings or their commercial interests—should have a voice in its affairs. The poor, who go to work as children, have little or no schooling, and have little or no spare time to pay attention to politics: hence they lack the competence that is prerequisite to suffrage.

In addition, the oligarchs clearly express their awareness of the threats to the establishment of this move by the Levellers to give the poor political equality with the rich. The appeal to natural rights, says Cromwell over and over again, leads to anarchy—calls for the overthrow of established legal rights and privileges. Even more dire is the threat to property itself; for as Ireton and Cromwell point out, when the poor, who are the many, have political equality with the rich, who are the few, what is to stop them from voting for measures that will tend to equalize the possession of wealth, by taking it from the rich and giving it to the poor?

To these two charges, especially to the second, the Levellers have no satisfactory answer, though they try to assure the rich that they have nothing to fear.

Almost two hundred years later, in 1821, a similar debate took place in the New York State Constitutional Convention. In that debate, Chancellor Kent, speaking for the landed gentry of upstate New York, plainly fearful of the teeming population of New York City, made up largely of immigrant and uneducated poor, pointed out that there can be no retreat from universal suffrage. He said:

Universal suffrage, once granted, is granted forever and never can be recalled. There is no retrograde step in the rear of democracy.

And he argued against it on the following grounds.

The apprehended danger from the experiment of universal suffrage applied to the whole legislative department is no dream of the imagination. It is too mighty an excitement for the moral constitution of men to endure. The tendency of universal suffrage is to jeopardize the rights of property and the principles of liberty.

His opponents, like those of Cromwell and Ireton, sought to assure him that their demands for political equality involved no threat to property and other legally established rights and privileges. (Once again it must be observed that when they use the words "all men" in speaking for universal suffrage, they plainly mean all white men—not human beings who are either black or female.)

In between these two debates, the readings of the first Monday introduce into the discussion an extraordinary paper by Benjamin Franklin, arguing that the minority of the rich should not be allowed to prevail over the majority of the poor because no special political wisdom attaches to the possession of wealth. In the course of his argument, Franklin makes what is, by far, the most radical statement—not only in his time, but for any time—about the rights of property. I quote.

Private property therefore is a creature of society and is subject to the calls of that society whenever its necessities shall require it, even to its last farthing; its contributions to the public exigencies are not to be considered as conferring a benefit on the public, entitling the contributors to the distinctions of honor and power, but as the return of an obligation previously received, or the payment of a just debt.

The fourth reading on the first Monday—the Declaration of Independence, which I hope you all know by heart, at least the first twenty lines of the second paragraph—appears to be silent on the conflict between the democrats and the oligarchs. Yet we are compelled to ask what is implied by such statements that all men are created equal, that all have certain unalienable rights, that among these is the right to liberty, and that free government and political liberty involve the consent of the governed. Our discussion of the Declaration usually leads to different interpretations of its meaning in the light of the issue that has been so clearly delineated by the debate in Cromwell's army, the debate in the New York State Constitutional Convention, and Franklin's paper on representation and property.

If I were to stop right here, having summarized no more than the materials for discussion on the first Monday, would you have any difficulty whatsoever in seeing the relevance of the Aspen Readings in the autumn of 1972, as the issues involved in the contest for the presidency are joined by the candidates? The readings for the first Monday have introduced all the basic concepts—equality, liberty, property, and justice in connection with the notion of rights. But as we now go on to Tuesday and Wednesday, you will see that much remains to be read and discussed to get these basic concepts clearer and to have a better grasp of the many related issues in which they are involved.

FIRST TUESDAY (second session)

R. H. Tawney: *Equality*, 1929

Henry George: *Progress and Poverty*, 1879

William Graham Sumner: *The Challenge of Facts*, 1890

John C. Calhoun: *On Constitutional Government*, 1831

Our discussion starts with Tawney, even though he is latest in time, because the chapter we read in his book on equality helps us to make the following distinctions that we need in order to get the issues about equality clarified. On the one hand, personal equality and inequality—an equality or inequality, comparing one individual with another, of endowments and attainments. On the other hand, equality and inequality of conditions—of the external circumstances under which we live, such as equality and inequality of social, political, and economic status or opportunity.

Tawney and Henry George also help us to see that the issue which divides the writers that we read for Tuesday is not the same as the issue which divided the writers we read for Monday. Yesterday, the question was: Shall those who are economically unequal—the rich and the poor, the propertied and unpropertied—be granted political equality by extending the franchise to the poor? But today, two hundred years or more after the debate of this issue in Cromwell's army, Tawney and George, living in societies in which suffrage has been greatly extended, if not yet universalized, pose a different question and raise a different issue.

The question they ask is: Now that suffrage has been extended to the working classes in the population, who are still both the poor and the many, must we not do something about making those who are politically equal—at least in their right to vote—also economically equal? Must we not narrow the gap between the economic power of the rich and the powerlessness of the poor in order to make the suffrage of the poor politically effective instead of a hollow sham?

Stated in other terms, the question is whether political democracy or political equality can be made to work unless it is also accompanied by economic democracy and equality? (The fears of Cromwell, Ireton, and Chancellor Kent, about the invasion of property rights as a consequence of giving the franchise to the poor, were not ill-founded.)

Tawney and George argue that the promotion of economic equality is absolutely indispensable to the effectiveness of political democracy. Listen to the words of Henry George.

Where there is anything like an equal distribution of wealth, the more democratic the government the better it will be; but where there is gross inequality in the distribution of wealth, the more democratic the government the worse it will be; for, while rotten democracy may not in itself be worse than rotten autocracy, its effects upon national character will be worse. To put political power in the hands of men embittered and degraded by poverty is to tie firebrands to foxes and turn them loose amid the standing corn; it is to put out the eyes of a Samson and to twine his arms around the pillars of national life.

Against them John Calhoun and William Graham Sumner argue that the creation of an equality of conditions—especially in the economic sphere—is the death of individual freedom. An equality of economic conditions cannot be produced without control of the economy by the central government, and this tends to reduce or eliminate freedom of enterprise. Liberty and equality cannot be reconciled, say both Sumner and Calhoun. Listen to the words of Calhoun.

There is another error, not less great and dangerous, usually associated with the one which has just been considered. I refer to the opinion that liberty and equality are so intimately united that liberty cannot be perfect without perfect equality.

That they are united to a certain extent and that equality of citizens, in the eyes of the law, is essential to liberty in a popular government is conceded. But to go further and make equality of condition essential to liberty would be to destroy both liberty and progress. The reason is that inequality of condition, while it is a necessary consequence of liberty, is, at the same time, indispensable to progress.

We have been confronted with a head-on collision between the proponents of a liberty that calls for equality and the proponents of a liberty that calls for inequality—the equality and inequality in both cases being economic. Can this issue be resolved? Is there any way of seeing around it?

Not without a better understanding of what is meant by economic equality. It is on this most difficult question that Tawney provides our discussion with the greatest help. He points out that there are only two possible meanings of economic equality. One is pecuniary equality, equality of possessions, equality of property or money in the bank—ultimately, an equality that is measured in *quantitative* terms. The other meaning is the economic equality of individuals who have whatever *any* human being needs in order to lead a decent human life—even though one man may have more than anyone needs, and another man may have just enough of what anyone needs. This is clearly a *qualitative* as opposed to a *quantitative* meaning of economic equality.

As we examine Tawney's pages carefully, we find that he thinks that it is utterly chimerical to attempt to establish economic equality in the quantitative sense; and that the ideal of economic equality, or of an economically classless society, can be realized only in qualitative terms; namely, that every human being shall have what any human being needs to lead a good life, even though some have more than that. As you might imagine, this leads to much questioning about human needs, and considerable disagreement about the realizability of economic equality in either sense of the term.

Nevertheless, the question of economic equality remains with us as we go on to the next day and the days thereafter. It involves two points. One is: Can political democracy be made to work if some members of the population have less than they need in the way of such economic goods as schooling, medical care, free time, recreation, etc.? The other is: Can it be made to work if some portion of the population has so much more than they need that this excess of wealth gives them undue political power and influence?

FIRST WEDNESDAY (third session)

Alexis de Tocqueville: *Democracy in America*, 1835

Theodore Roosevelt: *The New Nationalism*, 1910

The Progressive Party Platform, 1912

As the second day's discussion flows into the third, we find T. R. saying in 1910 what Henry George had said in 1879 and what Tawney will be saying in England twenty years later—that poverty, or the chasm between the rich and the poor, prevents the poor from making their influence felt in public affairs even when they had been granted suffrage and political equality with the rich. Listen to T. R. in 1910.

No man can be a good citizen unless he has a wage more than sufficient to cover the bare cost of living, and hours of labor short enough so that after his day's work is done he will have time and energy to bear his share in the management of the community, to help in carrying the general load. We keep countless men from being good citizens by the conditions of life with which we surround them.

But the problem that we are confronted with cannot be easily solved, as our reading of Tocqueville gradually makes us aware. In fact, as we slowly come to understand Tocqueville's controlling insights about democracy, we also slowly come to realize how terrifying is the problem that we face—and cannot avoid.

There is a bridge in our discussion, as we pass from Tawney on the second day to Tocqueville on the third. Our deepest understanding of what Tawney is driving at in his defense of the ideal of equality is reached when we see that what he is seeking is a truly classless society, in which all men are treated as equal without regard to the accidents of birth, possessions, occupations, or other circumstances that might divide them into antagonistic social or economic classes. Although Tocqueville does not use the phrase "classless society," we are able quickly to see that his conception of democracy as a society in which a universal equality of conditions is achieved—an equality of social, economic, and political conditions—is a truly classless society.

With that understood, we also understand Tocqueville to be saying that the kind of democracy—or equality of conditions—which he observed coming into being in America in 1835 is ordained by Divine Providence to spread and spread until it has become worldwide, everywhere replacing the ancient regime of aristocracy, inequality, and special privilege. But while Tocqueville is the prophet of the ascendancy of democratic institutions in human affairs, he is also filled with the gravest forebodings that the triumph of democracy may be accompanied by the destruction of freedom. He is, in short, sympathetic to Calhoun's proposition that individual liberty cannot be reconciled with an equality of conditions. In one of his most telling passages on the subject of liberty and equality, he writes:

I think that democratic communities have a natural taste for freedom; left to themselves, they will seek it, cherish it, and view any privation of it with regret. But for equality, their passion is ardent, insatiable, incessant, invincible; they call for equality in freedom, and, if they cannot obtain that, they still call for equality in slavery. They will endure poverty, servitude, barbarism; but they will not endure aristocracy.

His forebodings that democracy, most fully realized in an equality of conditions, especially economic conditions, may lead to despotism is expressed in a passage that puzzles us when we first read it. I quote.

I think, then, that the species of oppression by which democratic nations are menaced is unlike anything which ever before existed in the world; our contemporaries will find no prototype of it in their memories. I seek in vain for an expression which will accurately convey the whole of the idea I have formed of it; the old words "despotism" and "tyranny" are inappropriate. The thing itself is new, and since I cannot name, I must attempt to define it.

What is this new and most terrible form of tyranny and despotism for which Tocqueville cannot find a name? Suggestions of every sort emerge in the discussion at this point, until we finally realize that the name for which Tocqueville was searching did not become a generally accepted label until almost a hundred years later. It is *totalitarianism*. And then we begin to understand, from other passages that I do not have time to quote, that what Tocqueville was foreseeing is the rise of totalitarian democracy—paradoxical as that may sound.

With that insight, we pursue our discussion of Tocqueville; first, by trying to understand why an equality of conditions, especially economic conditions, can lead to a totalitarian state, in which the central government exercises complete power over the lives of individuals; and second, by trying to discover whether Tocqueville has any remedy for this—any way of preventing democracy from turning sour.

On the first point, Tocqueville leads us to see that in order to obtain and preserve an equality of conditions, the people tend to grant more and more power to the central government, which tends to become totalitarian when it approaches having a complete monopoly of both political and economic power. On the second point, Tocqueville does have a remedy to propose to us. I wish I had time to quote the magnificent passages that we ponder and dissect in the seminar, but I must summarize them briefly.

In the ancient regime, the power of the king was held in check by the countervailing power of the nobles—the aristocracy of various ranks and stations. The power of the king, says Tocqueville, did not bear down on the people with all its weight and force; for its downward thrust was broken by the power retained by what Tocqueville calls the local and secondary agencies of government, embodied in the dukes, counts, and barons. (This was the way things operated until Louis the Fourteenth emasculated the nobility and made himself the autocrat of France.) By analogy, Tocqueville suggests that a democracy, with equality of conditions, can still preserve individual liberty by giving countervailing power to secondary agencies of government, in the form of private associations or corporations of all sorts that are not creatures of the central government. To make this work, the institution of private property must be preserved and protected; for, without that, private corporations or associations cannot exercise effective power against the central government and prevent it from becoming the monolithic giant that turns the state into a totalitarian monstrosity.

Once again, in our third day of discussion, we are confronted with a crucial issue about liberty and equality, and one that also involves property and justice. On the one hand, we have T. R. in his New Nationalism speech, which calls for a Fair Deal, asking for increased power in the central government to check the power of the private corporations—for the sake of maximizing liberty and equality for all. On the other hand, we have Tocqueville warning us that that program might lead to the very opposite result; and that to preserve individual liberty while promoting economic and political equality, we must diminish or check the power of the central government, and do so by preserving the power of private corporations and associations as secondary agencies of government.

FIRST THURSDAY, FRIDAY, AND SATURDAY AND SECOND MONDAY (fourth through seventh sessions)

If I were to summarize in comparable detail what is to be learned from the readings assigned for these days and from the discussion of the texts read, this lecture would reach insufferable or at least exhausting proportions. Even so, I must tell you that the detail with which I have summarized the first three days does not do justice to all the points that are met with in the course of our discussions. I have read you only a small fraction of the passages that the participants in the seminar mark, try to interpret, and argue about. To follow the one thin line of discussion that I have chosen to make the theme of this lecture, I must get on to the readings of the eighth session—the second Tuesday.

Though I want to get there quickly, I cannot bring myself to leap-frog over four days of the seminar, with no mention at all of the readings and themes or problems that we discuss.

FIRST THURSDAY (fourth session)

Aristotle: *Politics*, Book I (4th century B.C.)

Rousseau: *The Social Contract*, Book I (18th century)

Here we have the basic questions about the origin and nature of civil society, the political community, or the state and its government, including questions about how government is compatible with freedom, under what conditions government is legitimate, what is involved in the distinction between despotic government and constitutional government, and in the distinction between being the subject of a despot and the citizen of a republic.

In the course of the discussion of these matters, another basic issue about equality emerges; namely, the issue whether, in fact, all men are equal—Aristotle holding that some men are by nature intended to be citizens and to exercise political freedom, while others are intended by nature to be slaves and to serve their masters; Rousseau holding the very opposite view—that all men are by nature intended for a life of freedom, and that it is nurture or circumstances, not nature, that makes some men appear to be slavish.

I cannot pass over this without reporting that in every seminar I have moderated, some participants, often a goodly number, finally find themselves in agreement with Aristotle rather than with Rousseau. *Make of that what you will!*

FIRST FRIDAY (fifth session)

Plato: *The Republic*, Books I and II

together with the Melian Dialogue from Thucydides' *History of the Peloponnesian War*, and

FIRST SATURDAY (sixth session)

Machiavelli: *The Prince*

I have bracketed these two days together because together these readings lead us into a discussion of the two great questions about what justice is and about justice and expediency.

The first of these questions is the easier of the two. A single line in Plato helps us to answer it—the line in which it is suggested that justice consists in giving to each man what is his due—what he has a rightful claim to. If this is not the whole answer, or if it involves further questions about what is due a man or what he has a rightful claim to, it is at least the beginning of an answer about what justice is.

The second question always leaves everyone puzzled because Plato poses it so forcefully and then does not provide even a clue to the answer in the texts that we read. The question is, why should I be just? What's in it for me? Will being just to others contribute to my own individual happiness? In short, is it expedient to be just?

The problem having thus been posed by Plato, we find ourselves increasingly puzzled by Machiavelli's recommendations to the prince about the expediency or inexpediency of being a virtuous ruler. Would it be expedient to be a just ruler if all or most men are bad? And are most men in fact bad, or are they for the most part bad? If so, what is the expedient thing to do in dealing with them? If not, is justice, after all, also expedient?

SECOND MONDAY (seventh session)

Sophocles: *Antigone* (5th century B.C.)

Melville: *Billy Budd* (19th century)

Martin Luther King: *Letter from a Birmingham Jail* (20th century)

I cannot possibly summarize the wonderfully intricate discussion of tragedy that these readings provoke and promote. There is time to make only one point here; namely, that when we understand the essence of tragedy as consisting in having to make an inescapable choice between equally evil alternatives, Martin Luther King's *Letter from a Birmingham Jail* opens our eyes to the tragic choice that confronts America today in the conflict between justice and expediency in the treatment of its black citizens.

These four days, over which I have jumped at high speed, all contribute to our understanding of the problems of democracy and capitalism in the 20th century, in ways that I have not had time to point out. Without further ado, I now turn to the remaining five days, in which we deal with questions about liberty in relation to law and government, and with basic problems concerning the production and distribution of wealth and the ownership of property. The questions about liberty occur on the second Tuesday.

SECOND TUESDAY (eighth session)

John Locke: *Second Treatise on Civil Government*, 1689

Jonathan Boucher: *On Civil Liberty*, 1775

John Stuart Mill: *On Liberty*, 1863

The two questions that control our discussion of these three texts are first, whether there is one or several conceptions of liberty presented in the pages that we have read; and second, if there are several, how they differ in their understanding of the relation of liberty to law and government. The exploration of these questions reflects backward upon the problems we have been facing concerning the relation of liberty and equality as well as the distinctions we have been considering concerning the kinds of government. The quickest way, perhaps, to summarize what can be learned from the reading and discussion of these materials is to catch what is central and pivotal in the views of each of the three authors.

Jonathan Boucher, first—a Tory preacher in the American colonies trying to persuade his congregation not to rebel against their King and Parliament. His view of government is that the king rules by divine right as vicar of

God on earth. He has read John Locke's *Second Treatise* and will have no truck with all this talk about freedom under government being derived from the consent of the governed, or about unalienable natural rights, including the right to dissent or even to rebel. Freedom, for Boucher, consists not in doing as one pleases, but only in doing as one ought; and since the law—the law of God or the law of the King—lays down what one ought or ought not to do, freedom consists in acting in accordance with the law. The spheres of law and of liberty—of conduct regulated by law and of conduct that manifests freedom—coincide perfectly. All else is license, i.e., doing as one pleases is not liberty, but license.

Boucher stands out at one extreme and, by consulting our texts, we soon find that J. S. Mill—the great exponent of liberalism in the 19th century—stands at the opposite pole. Freedom, according to Mill, consists in doing what one pleases provided that in so doing we do no injury to others or to the community. Since the law aims to proscribe conduct that is injurious—harmful to the community or to its members, the individual who behaves lawfully—who obeys the law—is, in doing so, not free. Neither is the criminal who disobeys the law; criminal behavior is license, not liberty. Where Boucher made the spheres of law and liberty perfectly coincident, Mill makes them absolutely exclusive. This strikes us most forcefully when we find the passage in which he says that as the sphere of law enlarges, the sphere of liberty diminishes, and conversely. The more things are regulated by law and government, the less free we are; and so, as one who wishes to maximize human freedom, Mill calls for as little government as possible—no more than is needed to do for society what its individuals or its private associations cannot do for themselves. (In our discussion of Mill, we cannot avoid noting how much a nineteenth-century liberal sounds like a twentieth-century Goldwater conservative.)

Our discussion, having located the polar extremes, now tries to find the middle ground between them. It is occupied by John Locke. His position becomes clear as we observe that, for him, freedom takes three distinct forms.

First, there is political liberty, the liberty of the citizen who is governed only with his consent and who also, through the exercise of suffrage, has a voice in his own government. (This, we recall, is the liberty that Aristotle first conceived when he spoke of constitutional government as the government of free men and equals—each a citizen having a share of the sovereignty and a voice in his own government.)

Second, there is liberty under law. According to Locke, a man is free when he obeys a law established by a government to which he has given his consent, and in the making of which law he has exercised a voice through suffrage. (We note how different this conception of liberty under law is from Boucher's conception of it. The subject of an absolute monarch, obeying his edicts, would be acting as a free man, according to Boucher; but not according to Locke. Only the consenting citizen with suffrage is free when he acts in obedience to law.)

Third, there is the freedom to do as one pleases in all matters about which the law is silent; or, as Locke says, "in all matters where the law prescribes not."

With all these distinctions on the table, the discussion pulls some things together that have been up in the air for several days. Someone always asks how it can be said that a man is free when he obeys a law that is contrary to hi wishes. He has opposed the making of that law; but it has been made a law by the majority, and he belongs to the adversely affected minority. How is such a man free? If he is not free, someone else always observes, then majority rule, under a constitutional government, involves a deprivation of freedom for minorities—as much of a deprivation of freedom as is suffered by the subjects of an absolute monarch.

The difference then begins to become clear. The subject of an absolute monarch is ruled without his consent and without participation through suffrage. But the citizen of a republic has given his consent to the constitution or the framework of government, and also to the principle of decision by majorities; he has, therefore, agreed in advance to the legitimacy of a law that is both constitutional and also has the support of the majority. In that case, such a law is a law of his own making, even though he may have voted against it or wished it not to become law. The adversely affected minority is, therefore, as free under the law as the majority who enacted it.

This does not mean, of course, that a majority cannot misrule and that one or another minority cannot be oppressed by such misrule. But we also come to discover that the only remedy for majority misrule is the American invention of a judicial review of legislation. In the case of despotic misrule the only remedy is rebellion.

At the conclusion of our conversation about these matters, I cannot refrain from calling attention to an insight that has emerged from such discussions in many years of Aspen seminars. Our century has witnessed a revolutionary change that is like a continental divide or watershed in history. In all preceding centuries, social, political, or eco-

nomic injustice always took the form of the exploitation
of the many by the few—misrule by a minority, oppression of the majority. In our century, for the first time, the
situation is radically reversed in all our constitutional de-
mocracies: now, such injustice as exists takes the form of
misrule by the majority and the oppression of one or another minority.

The portent or prospect for the future that we see here
is the elimination of conflict between the opposed interests
of majorities and minorities, with the achievement of a society that is more truly classless than any that now exists—a society from which all class conflict has been
removed. One other pointer to be learned from this is that
rebellion against misrule is more difficult to mount and has
less chance of success when the impulse to rebel motivates
a minority instead of a majority.

SECOND WEDNESDAY (ninth session)

On this occasion, we return to three authors that we
have already read—to Aristotle's *Politics*, Rousseau's *Social
Contract*, and Locke's *Second Treatise of Civil Government*.
But now the selections that we read are not about the state
and government, or about liberty and equality, but about
an idea that we had not yet explored to any extent—the
idea of property, and, with it, all the questions concerning
the right to ownership, the production and distribution of
wealth and—once again—the ideas of economic justice and
economic equality.

The text that lays the groundwork for our discussion is
Chapter 5 of Locke's *Treatise*—the chapter on property.
We will find that the basic points of his analysis are confirmed in Chapter 9 of Book I of Rousseau's *Social Contract*. Some additional insights will be derived from our

consideration of what Aristotle has to say about the acquisition and pursuit of wealth in the closing chapters of the first book of his *Politics*.

What are Locke's basic points? They are, first, that every man has a natural right to property in his own person. He owns his own body and mind and all their powers; they belong to him by birthright. The ownership by one man of another as a chattel slave is a violation of this natural right. Second, the opposite of natural property is that which is originally *common* to all men—the earth and all its resources. We then come, third, to Locke's great formulation of the labor theory of property.

When an individual mixes his own labor power (of mind or body) with that which is common, the product of that mixture is rightfully his; or, in other words, a man has a right to that which he produces by the application of his labor power to that which is common. The product is rightfully acquired property.

The members of the group immediately call attention to two limitations that Locke then places on the acquisition of property. One is that the producer must not appropriate more than he can consume or more than he needs: he must not acquire a surplus that is wasted or unused. The other limitation is that he must not appropriate so much from the common that not enough is left for others to acquire by their labor for their needs.

So far, so good. The points just made seem sound and unobjectionable. But as we explore the text further—and more carefully—we come upon two serious difficulties that leave us quite up in the air, and open the door to discussions that must take place in the days to follow.

The first difficulty is fully understood only after we grapple with the following passage:

He that is nourished by the acorns he picked up under an oak, or the apples he gathered from the trees in the wood, has certainly appropriated them to himself. . . . And it is plain, if the first gathering made them not his, nothing else could. That labour put a distinction between them and common. That added something to them more than Nature, the common mother of all, had done, and so they became his private right. . . . Thus, the grass my horse has bit, the turfs my servant has cut, and the ore I have digged in any place, where I have a right to them in common with others, become my property without the assignation or consent of anybody. The labour that was mine, removing them out of that common state they were in, hath fixed my property in them.

The ore that I have digged is mine by my own labor power. But what about the grass my horse has bit, or the turf my servant has cut? Here, we soon realize, is the first appearance of capital and labor as related factors in the production of wealth. My servant is a hired hand, a wage-laborer. My horse, which I may own through having captured him and tamed him, is capital that I have rightfully acquired. Suppose, now, that I do no work myself, but put to work my horse (my capital) and my servant (a laborer whose wages I have paid). Can I rightfully claim possession of the product of these two factors—one of which I own (the horse) and the other of which I have paid off (the laborer)? The import of that question becomes clear enough for us to realize that we had better table it for discussion later when we have read the labor papers scheduled for Thursday, and the *Communist Manifesto* scheduled for Friday.

The second difficulty hits us when we find Locke saying that his own sensible limitations on the acquisition of wealth are set aside by the invention of money, in the form of relatively imperishable pieces of metal. Since coin satisfies no natural need, as food, shelter, and clothing do, it is not subject to the injunction that a man should restrain himself from acquiring more than he needs. And since it is relatively imperishable, as consumable commodities are not, it does not spoil or waste.

Locke offers no solution of this difficulty; he apparently sees no way to impose restraints on the accumulation of wealth in the form of money or coin. At this very point, however, Aristotle has something to say—on this very same problem about the limited or limitless acquisition of wealth. We observe his distinction between natural and artificial wealth—natural wealth in the form of consumable commodities; artificial wealth in the form of money, which should serve only as a medium of exchange.

In the light of this distinction, Aristotle, the moralist, keeps reminding us that our aim is not just to live, but to live well; and so we should not accumulate wealth endlessly but only as much as we need in order to lead a good life. The discussion at this point opens up questions about virtue and happiness, individual wants and natural needs—ethical questions the importance of which we recognize but which we cannot pursue at length. Yet they will hover around us in the subsequent sessions as we deal with the more strictly economic questions that the readings of the next few days raise for us.

SECOND THURSDAY (tenth session)
Alexander Hamilton: *Report on Manufacturers*, 1790

Boston Carpenter's Strike, 1825

Preamble of the Mechanics Union of Philadelphia, 1827

On this occasion, the focus of our discussion is the incredibly remarkable document known as the *Preamble of the Mechanics Union*, published in Philadelphia by American workmen some twenty years before Marx and Engels published the *Communist Manifesto*. Before I report the things that we learn from reading and discussing it, I must call attention to a few things that we come to see in the light of the other documents assigned for this session.

Hamilton's arguments in favor of the greater productivity of an industrial or manufacturing economy, as compared with a nonindustrial agricultural economy, cause us to consider the factors that can make one economy more productive than another.

Let us consider two economies in which the only factors in the production of wealth are laborers and hand-tools. The economy with more hands and hand-tools will be the more productive. Now let us consider two economies, each of which has an equal supply of hands or manpower, but one of which has, in addition, productive machinery, driven by power other than human or animal power. In this case, Hamilton argues, the economy in which production involves machinery will clearly be the more productive, because the addition of machines can be equated to an increase in labor power, or the number of hands.

We find it useful at this point to introduce the terms "laboristic" and "capitalistic" as terms descriptive of the way in which wealth is produced, without any regard to how the instruments of its production are owned. An economy is laboristic in its mode of production if its wealth is produced mainly by human labor, aided only by hand-tools and domesticated animals. An economy is capitalistic in its mode of production if its wealth is produced by the combination of human labor with power-driven machinery and other capital instruments of production.

With this distinction before us, we see that Hamilton was saying that, in a capitalistic economy, more wealth can be produced with less labor power; and that, as capital instruments become more and more powerful productive forces, the same amount of wealth can be produced with fewer and fewer hands.

The document that records the Boston Carpenter's Strike of 1825 presents statements by three parties: the journeymen—carpenters, who are wage-laborers; the master-carpenters, whom today we would call the managers; and the gentlemen engaged in building—clearly the capitalists, or owners of the means of production. The demands of labor, in this very early instance of a labor strike, are for higher wages and for shorter hours; and the purpose of the latter demand is not only to acquire more free time for themselves but also to increase the opportunity for the employment of others who at the moment are out of work. The managers and the capitalists respond to these demands by saying that higher wages are out of the question. As for shorter hours, that is not good for the workmen because it will lead them into idleness and vice. It never occurs to them that they themselves have plenty of free time on their hands, and that if the workmen had been given schooling, they, too, could use the free time for the pursuits of leisure, and not be corrupted by idleness or vice.

When, a few years later, the Philadelphia Mechanics made similar demands—for higher wages and shorter hours—they specifically make this point, that they want more free time in order to engage in the pursuits of leisure that are so essential to the leading of a good human life. But that is not what we find most striking—and most troubling—in the *Preamble* which, by the way, echoes the high rhetorical tone of the *Declaration of Independence*. It is a very rich and subtle text to read and study, and by working at it we discover points that anticipate the *Communist Manifesto* by twenty years.

The most obvious of these is the argument that unless the capitalists, who are few, increase the purchasing power of the laborers, who are many, the increased productivity of an industrial economy will result in overproduction and underconsumption, with consequent economic crises for the capitalists as well as the workers. All questions of justice aside, the Philadelphia Mechanics point out to the capitalists that raising wages is to their self-interest as a matter of expediency, for the increased purchasing power of labor will enable workmen to buy more of the goods— luxuries as well as necessities—that the capitalists want to sell.

This is quickly seen as an anticipation of Henry Ford's reason for raising the wages of the workmen in his Detroit plant; and, in a way, it is also an anticipation of Marx's prediction that, if the capitalists continue in their policy of paying bare subsistence wages, bourgeois capitalism will sow the seeds of its own destruction, for the successive cycles of boom and bust will end in one grand bust, or collapse of the whole system through overproduction and underconsumption.

With some effort at a very close reading of the text, we

next uncover in the arguments advanced two contradictions that set the stage for our discussion of the *Communist Manifesto*.

The first is as follows. On the one hand, the mechanics claim that labor is the sole source of wealth, the only factor at work in its production, and that the capitalists, the owners of the means of production, contribute nothing at all. On the other hand, instead of asking for the whole pie—all the wealth produced—they ask only for their fair share. If, in fact, capitalists are unproductive, and labor is the only productive factor, then no return should go to capital, and all should go to labor.

The second contradiction is as follows. Though, as we have seen, the mechanics claim that labor is the sole source of wealth, the only productive factor, we find them conceding, in one passage after another, that the increased productivity of the society in which they live is to be attributed to the increased power of the machines that have resulted from modern science and technology. In fact, they point out that these powerful machines have steadily diminished the demand for labor. That certainly is inconsistent with their claim that labor is the only productive force, the sole factor operative in the production of wealth.

I said, a moment ago, that these two contradictions set the stage for our discussion of Marx, for they bear directly on the central issue concerning the labor theory of value and the role of the capitalist in the production of wealth. But before we go forward to the consideration of that issue, let us look backward briefly at the bearing of these contradictions on what we learned from our discussion of Locke's labor theory of property—not the same as Marx's labor theory of value

Let us reconsider the man who, by his own labor, fenced

in some land, and then, again by his own labor, caught a wild horse and tamed and trained him. Another man comes by his plot of land and freely contracts to work for him for a certain compensation. Does the man who rightfully owns the land and the horse, and pays another to work for him on his land and with his horse, contribute to production even though he does no further work himself?

According to the labor theory of value, which holds that labor is the only factor in the production of wealth, the non-working capitalist (owner of the horse and land and employer—or exploiter—of labor) is non-productive and so should receive no return whatsoever. But if the opposite theory is true, maintaining that there are two distinct factors in production—labor and capital, then the owner of capital contributes to production when he puts his capital to work even though he does no work himself; and so he should receive a share of the wealth produced, proportionate to the contribution made by his investment of capital. There is, of course, much more to say about all this, but it must wait for the final Friday and Saturday, to which we now turn.

SECOND FRIDAY (eleventh session)

Marx and Engels: *The Communist Manifesto*, 1848

Horace Mann: *The Importance of Universal, Free, Public Education*, 1854

Charles H. Vail: *The Socialist Movement*, 1903

We find that Marx and Engels are more rigorous in their statement of the labor theory of value than the Philadelphia Mechanics, and that they do not hesitate to draw the only conclusion that can be drawn from that premise, instead of contradicting themselves.

All wealth is produced by labor; the capital instruments used by laborers are themselves nothing but congealed labor; the owner of the capital instruments who does not work himself is totally unproductive and, making no contribution, should receive no part of the wealth produced. Any profit that he takes from the use of his capital is unearned increment and represents an exploitation of labor that is simply thievery.

That, we are able to discover by a close reading of a few pages, is the argument in a nutshell. And in a few paragraphs more, we find: that for all the wealth produced by labor to be enjoyed only by labor, it is necessary to abolish the private ownership of capital, and to turn its ownership over to the community itself, the collective body known as the state; and the state will then become the sole distributor of the wealth produced, taking, as the slogan goes, from each according to his abilities, and giving to each according to his needs.

There is still a step in the argument that is not sufficiently clear. We keep asking what it means to say that the capital instruments are congealed labor and that, therefore, they should not be privately owned. The little essay by Charles Vail, an early American socialist, helps us to get a little better understanding of this point.

Vail points out that when hand tools were privately produced by the individual workman and privately operated by him in his individual efforts, it was quite proper for such tools to be privately owned, and the fruit of their productivity to be privately acquired. But, Vail goes on, modern industrial capital is socially produced and socially operated. It is socially produced in the sense that the science and technology from which it originates is the product of human society as a whole over the centuries. It is socially operated in the sense that it requires an organized labor force to put it to work. Therefore, Vail argues, being socially produced and socially operated, it should be socially owned—by the collectivity or the state—and the wealth it produces should be socially distributed by the state.

At this point, objections begin to arise from many directions. I will only mention some of the most telling. Is capital socially produced? Are not the science and technology that go into the invention of industrial capital knowledge that exists in the public domain? Is it not like Locke's *common*, open to appropriation by anyone who has enough enterprise and ingenuity to make productive use of it? If so, then that argument against the private ownership of capital fails.

If the capital has been fairly acquired by the enterprise of the capitalist, and if the capitalist then pays laborers the wages they demand as fair compensation for their labor, the production of wealth would seem to involve more than the one factor of labor, in the form of living or congealed labor. It would seem to involve a quite distinct productive factor—capital instruments in the form of natural resources and industrial machinery. The private owner of capital would, then, appear to be a producer, even if he does not work himself; and as a producer he would be entitled to his share of the wealth produced.

With these questions and objections raised, the discussion returns to the text of the *Communist Manifesto* to take note of an inconsistency that opens a new line of thought for us.

On the one hand, Marx alleges that it is the private ownership of the means of production that causes the exploitation of labor and the misery of the proletariat. That being the cause, the remedy is clear: abolish the private ownership of capital. The famous statement of this matter reads as follows.

The distinguishing feature of Communism is not the abolition of property generally, but the abolition of bourgeois property. But modern bourgeois private property is the final and most complete expression of the system of producing and appropriating products that is based on class antagonisms, on the exploitation of the many by the few.

In this sense the theory of the Communists may be summed up in the single sentence: abolition of private property.

But just one page later, we come upon another statement that we always read aloud in the seminar and that I will now read to you.

You are horrified at our intending to do away with private property. But in your existing society private property is already done away with for nine-tenths of the population; its existence for the few is solely due to its non-existence in the hands of those nine-tenths. You reproach us, therefore, with intending to do away with a form of property, the necessary condition for whose existence is the non-existence of any property for the immense majority of society.

In a word, you reproach us with intending to do away with your property. Precisely so; that is just what we intend.

Did you hear what that said, and do you understand what it implies? It said that less than one-tenth of the population owns the means of production. For the other nine-tenths or more, private property in the means of production has already been done away with by the vast accumulations acquired by a relatively few capitalists.

A moment's thought will discover what is implied; namely, that the cause of economic injustice or inequity is not the private ownership of capital, but rather the concentration of such private ownership in the hands of a few. But if that is the case, rather than private ownership itself, then the remedy is not the abolition of private ownership, but rather overcoming its concentration by diffusing the ownership of capital.

The Marxist remedy is exactly the opposite. The ownership of all means of production by the state is even more concentrated than its ownership by the few under bourgeois capitalism. And at this point we cannot help recalling Tocqueville's prediction of the consequences of concentrating all economic and political power in the hands of the central government and its bureaucrats—a totalitarian state in which all workers may be equal but in which none is free.

If the ideal is the classless society, or at least a society devoid of serious class conflicts, and one the members of which are not only equal but free, then, surprising as it may seem, it is the American educator, Horace Mann, not Karl Marx who gives us the formula for achieving the ideal. It is expressed in a single line in the little essay that is part of our reading on this occasion.

Capital and labor in different classes are essentially antagonistic; but capital and labor in the same class are essentially fraternal.

What that suggests is a republic in which all the citizens derive their income partly from the profits of capital and partly from the wages of labor: every man both a citizen and a capitalist, in an economy that preserves private property and free enterprise.

The discussion has now reached the point where it is possible to distinguish four forms of capitalism, and then to ask which of these forms is most supportive of political democracy and individual freedom. The four forms can be named and briefly described as follows.

1. *Bourgeois or nineteenth-century capitalism*, which now exists only in such backward countries as Saudi Arabia or Bolivia, and in which the ownership of capital is in the hands of the very few, with little or no participation by the many in economic welfare.

2. *State capitalism, otherwise known as communism*, in which the state owns all the means of production and distributes the wealth in such a way that all participate to some extent in the general economic welfare.

3. *Socialized capitalism, or the mixed economy*, as we know it in the United States, in England, in the Scandinavian countries, and so on, in which there is both a private sector and a public sector, some degree of private ownership and free enterprise, accompanied by elaborate government measure to ensure a welfare distribution.

4. *Diffused or universal capitalism*, the economy that is implicit in the formula proposed by Horace Mann, but does not yet exist, in which participation in the general economic welfare would be achieved by the ownership of capital rather than by welfare measures controlled and operated by the central government.

The question to be answered is: If you had your choice, which of these four forms of capitalism would you prefer as the economic underpinning of political democracy? Which do you think would establish both political and economic equality without sacrificing either political liberty or individual freedom?

Everything that we have learned in all the preceding days of our discussion now comes critically to bear on the choice of the answer. We have one more day and one more reading to help us decide—each man for himself in his own way, but obligated to give reasons for his choice.

SECOND SATURDAY (twelfth session)

John Strachey: *The Challenge of Democracy*

I wish there were time to indicate how this final reading helps us to tie together all the threads of our preceding discussions, but *not* in such a way that the issues with which we have been wrestling are resolved and we are left with certain conclusions on which we all agree. Instead, I must content myself with making the following few brief points.

John Strachey who, at one time, was a leading member of the British Communist Party and a renowned exponent of Marxist doctrine, reverses himself in this posthumously published essay, in which he argues that political democracy and the mixed economy come much nearer than communism to achieving the ideal that communism claims for itself—a relatively classless society, with freedom and equality for all, together with a large measure of economic welfare for all.

Strachey's very persuasive arguments do not prevent the discussion on this final day from reconsidering such questions as whether the mixed economy can solve the problem of its built-in inflationary spiral; whether its goal of full employment is not a misleading objective; and whether, by its very nature, the mixed economy is an unstable mixture that must resolve itself either by enlarging the public sector at the expense of the private, or move in the reverse direction away from greater and greater concentration of power in the central government.

Strachey, we observe, remains a Marxist at heart even though he appears to favor the socialized capitalism of a representative democracy rather than the totalitarianism of state capitalism—or communism. We note particularly the passage in which he says:

In one way or another, the people of the advanced democratic societies will arrange the distribution of the national income to suit themselves. Experience shows that they can do this in a number of ways. The most obvious of these ways is so to arrange the tax structure that the main fruits of production do not go to the owners but are shared, directly or indirectly, with the mass of the population.

We cannot help observing how clearly this echoes a famous passage at the close of the *Communist Manifesto*.

The first step in the revolution by the working class is to raise the proletariat to the position of the ruling class—to establish democracy.

That is what the Levellers were calling for when, in 1647, they demanded an extension of the franchise to those who owned no property. But, we then observe, Marx goes on to say:

The proletariat will use its political supremacy to wrest by degrees all capital from the bourgeoisie, to centralize all instruments of production in the hands of the state . . . , and to increase the total of productive forces as rapidly as possible.

Of course, in the beginning this cannot be effected except by means of despotic inroads on the rights of property and on the conditions of bourgeois production; by means of measures, therefore, which appear economically insufficient and untenable, but which, in the course of the movement outstrip themselves, necessitate further inroads upon the old social order, and are unavoidable as a means of entirely revolutionizing the mode of production.

The measures, which Marx then enumerates, involve such things as "a heavy progressive or graduated income tax," "abolition of all right of inheritance," state ownership of the means of production—the very things that Cromwell and Ireton, back in 1647, feared would happen if the franchise were extended to include the many who are poor and without property. We have come full cycle but with a reverse twist: in the three hundred years since the debate in Cromwell's army, the many are now well-off and politically powerful, and the few are no longer at the top but at the bottom. This raises questions on which the Aspen Readings may throw light but which they cannot answer.

APPENDIX III

SEMINARS FOR YOUNG PEOPLE—AN ESSENTIAL INGREDIENT IN BASIC SCHOOLING

(excerpts from an article published in *The American School Board Journal*, January 1982)

I

What are the essential ingredients for setting up seminars for young people involving great books and great ideas and aiming at intellectual discipline and philosophical thought? Let me, first, enumerate the external conditions that must be present; and after that I will describe briefly what the teacher—or moderator of the seminar, a better name for it—must do.

(1) The group should consist of no more than 20 or 25 students, ages anywhere from 12 to 18, all of whom are able to read above the 6th grade level.

(2) The seminar must run for at least two hours. It cannot be conducted in the usual 50 minute class session.

(3) The participants must be seated around a hollow square table large enough to accommodate all of them comfortably and in a way that enables them to see one another as well as the moderator and to talk around the table and across it. Such seminars cannot be conducted in ordinary classrooms with a teacher standing in front of the room and the students sitting in rows in front of the instructor.

(4) The so-called teacher or instructor should not regard himself as a teacher or instructor in the usual sense of those words. To do so is to fail miserably. For such a seminar to be successful, it must be carried on as a discussion among

equals with the leader or moderator of the discussion superior only in the following respects: a little older; a little better reader, having done more reading, and with a better disciplined mind.

These points of superiority should never become too manifest or the seminar will degenerate from a discussion among equals, which it should be, into a didactic session in which teacher tells students what he knows or understands and acts as if they were there to imbibe his views without questioning them.

The discussion leader or moderator must imitate Socrates—especially the calculated irony with which Socrates pretends not to know the right answers to the questions that are the backbone of the ongoing inquiry, in which Socrates himself is simply the principal inquirer, first among equals.

(5) Finally, what is needed for such seminars are reading materials that satisfy the following conditions: (a) they should be, unlike textbooks, over the heads of the students so that they have to struggle and stretch to understand them; (b) they should be relatively short in length, seldom more than 50 pages for a given occasion and usually less than thirty, so that they can be read through a number of times very carefully, marked, and annotated; (c) while short in length, they must be very rich in content, so that the topics they discuss and the issues they raise, will support two hours of discussion; (d) they must, therefore, be essentially philosophical texts, not merely factual or informational; i.e., they must deal with ideas and raise questions that cannot ever be answered by empirical or experimental investigation, by historical research, or by going to an encyclopaedia to look up the facts or get the information; in other words, the reading

and discussion should aim at improved understanding, not increased knowledge.

If all five of these external requirements cannot be fully satisfied, there is no point in undertaking such seminars.

If the administration of a school is so inflexible that it cannot break through its rigid routine of 50-minute class sessions conducted in ordinary classrooms, that school is no place for such seminars.

If instructors cannot be found who are willing to give up being teachers in the ordinary sense (teachers who teach by telling instead of by asking) or if instructors cannot be found who are willing to try to imitate Socrates, then such seminars should not be attempted.

I greatly fear that there are many schools—too many— that cannot or will not meet all the conditions I have laid down. But there are no schools at all anywhere in our country in which some of the conditions do not already exist or cannot be fulfilled. In any school system there are always enough students who can participate profitably in such seminars; and the reading materials required are always available.

II

I now come to the heart of the matter. If all the external conditions I have mentioned are fully satisfied, what remains to be specified is the role of the moderator of such seminars. What should he or she do and how should he or she do it?

(1) First and most important of all, the moderator must prepare for the conduct of such seminars by reading the work assigned as carefully as possible, with pencil in hand, underlining all the crucial words whose precise meaning must be kept in mind; marking the pivotal sentences or

paragraphs in which the author states his underlying theses succinctly, argues for them, or raises questions about them; and making marginal notes of all sorts about the connections between one part of the text and another.

(2) Next, the moderator must make a series of random notes about all the important points, questions, issues, that occur to him as materials for discussion.

(3) Then, carefully examining these random notes, the moderator should put down a very small number of questions, phrased with the greatest of care, that are to be the backbone of a two-hour discussion. Sometimes just one question will suffice for the whole two hours; sometimes three or four are needed; seldom, if ever, more than five.

If more than one, the questions must then be ordered so that the first opens up matter to be further explored by the second; the second leads to further explorations by the third question; and so on. In addition, the questions must be such that everyone in the group can be called upon to answer them; and the best opening question is one that everyone around the table is required to answer in succession.

(4) The moderator must never be satisfied with the answers given. The moderator must always ask, Why? No answer must be allowed to go by without having reasons offered in its support.

(5) The moderator should never allow any student, even one who appears to be thinking and trying to answer the question, to get away with slovenly speech—speech that is no more than a gurgle of words flung at the question with the hope that some of them may hit the target.

The moderator should relentlessly demand that the student's answer to a question posed should be phrased so that it aims at the bull's eye; that the student's statement is grammatically correct in every detail; that the student speak in clearly defined sentences and even in well-formulated paragraphs.

Above all, the moderator should never allow a single critical word to be used ambiguously or loosely. No one can legislate about how words should be used; but if two students use a given word in different senses, or if a student uses a word used by the author or by the moderator in a different sense, that difference in senses should be plainly recognized and labelled before the discussion proceeds another inch.

(6) The moderator should insist upon relevance in the answering of the questions asked. By this I mean no more than that the student attempt to answer the question, and not simply respond to it by blurting out whatever happens to be on his or her mind at the time.

A question addressed to a student is not like the ringing of a bell which indicates to the student that it is now his or her turn to speak and invites him or her to say anything he or she wishes, whether it is an answer to the question or not.

(7) If it appears from the way the question is being answered that the students do not really understand the question, the moderator must repeat the question in as many different ways as possible in an effort to be sure that the question is uniformly understood by all. There is no point in going on unless that is accomplished. The moderator may have to use a wide variety of concrete examples to get the question clear.

Asking the same question in a variety of ways and accompanying it by a diversity of illustrations requires great intellectual energy upon the part of the moderator. Conducting seminars is far from being an easy or passive performance, in which the moderator acts merely as chairman of a meeting at which the participants are invited to say anything they have on their minds.

(8) As the discussion gets going, conflicting answers to a given question will begin to emerge, and then the moderator must make everyone explicitly aware of the issue that is being joined. Unless it is clearly formulated and fully understood, debate of the issue cannot be carried on.

To aid such formulation and debate, the moderator should use the blackboard, putting on it some form of schematic diagram that frames the issue and indicates the opposing positions on it, so that the students can identify the position they are taking or the view they are defending.

With repeated experiences of seminars about the same bit of reading, the moderator will learn in advance how to construct such diagrams and can often put them on the blackboard before the discussion begins. When thus presented in a schematic form, the diagrams will employ symbols that will at first appear to be mere hieroglyphics to the student and will only become intelligible after the discussion has reached a certain point.

(9) The seminar should not attempt to reach conclusions about which everyone agrees. On the contrary, it should leave the students with an understanding of questions to be answered and problems to be solved. The understanding of the questions and of the range of answers they elicit are the important things, not this or that answer, however true or profound.

(10) In a succession of seminars, whatever understanding has been achieved in an earlier seminar should be used

in dealing with questions or issues raised in later seminars. Therefore, a useful ordering of the reading materials is just as important as the proper selection of them in the first place.

(11) The moderator must never talk down to the students or treat them as most teachers do when they are sitting in front of them in fifty minute class sessions. The moderator must make the greatest effort to understand what is going on in the mind of another human being who, even though much younger, is struggling to understand something that is difficult for anyone, including the moderator, to understand.

(12) The moderator must be patient and polite in dealing with everyone around the table, as patient and polite as one should be with guests at one's dinner table. The moderator should try to set an example of intellectual etiquette that the participants are induced to imitate. Above all, the moderator should conduct the whole discussion with a smile and try to produce laughter at as many points as possible. Nothing is more productive of learning than wit and laughter.

III

Here is a list of reading materials arranged in roughly chronological order, from which different selections can be made and set in different orders or sequences, depending on the number of seminars to be conducted in succession.

Plato: *The Apology*
      The Republic, Books I and II
Aristotle: *Ethics*, Book I
        Politics, Book I, together with Rousseau, *The Social Contract*, Book I

Marcus Aurelius, *Meditations*, together with Epictetus, *Enchiridion*

Lucretius, *On the Nature of Things*, Books I–IV

Plutarch's *Lives*, Alexander and Caesar

Augustine's *Confessions*, Books I–VIII

Montaigne's *Essays* (selected essays, all short)

Machiavelli, *The Prince* (selected chapters, short)

Locke, *Second Treatise on Civil Government*, Chapters I–V

The Declaration of Independence, the Preamble to the Constitution of the United States, and Lincoln's Gettysburg Address

Hamilton, Madison, Jay, *The Federalist*, Chapters I–X

J. S. Mill, *Essay on Representative Government* (selected chapters)

Melville, *Billy Budd*, together with Sophocles, *Antigone*